DEFEND YOURSELF

Biblical tactics for tearing down strongholds

DEFEND YOURSELF

CARA STARNS

Defend Yourself: Biblical Tactics for Tearing Down Strongholds

Copyright © 2022 by Cara Starns. All rights reserved.

No parts of this book may be reproduced, distributed, or transmitted in any form or by any means, without written permission from the copyright holder, except for brief quotations in printed or broadcasted reviews.

All Scripture quotations, unless otherwise indicated, are taken from the Holy Bible, New International Version®, NIV®. Copyright ©1973, 1978, 1984, 2011 by Biblica, Inc.® Used by permission of Zondervan. All rights reserved worldwide. www.zondervan.com

Scriptures marked KJV are taken from the KING JAMES VERSION (KJV): KING JAMES VERSION, public domain.

Scriptures marked AMP are taken from the AMPLIFIED BIBLE: Scripture taken from the AMPLIFIED® BIBLE, Copyright © 1954, 1958, 1962, 1964, 1965, 1987 by the Lockman Foundation Used by Permission. (www.Lockman.org)

Scriptures marked NKJV are taken from the NEW KING JAMES VERSION (NKJV): Scripture taken from the NEW KING JAMES VERSION®. Copyright© 1982 by Thomas Nelson, Inc. Used by permission. All rights reserved.

Scripture quotations marked NLT are taken from the Holy Bible, New Living Translation (NLT), copyright ©1996, 2004, 2015 by Tyndale House Foundation. Used by permission of Tyndale House Publishers, Carol Stream, Illinois 60188. All rights reserved.

Scripture quotations marked MSG are taken from THE MESSAGE, copyright © 1993, 2002, 2018 by Eugene H. Peterson. Used by permission of NavPress, represented by Tyndale House Publishers. All rights reserved.

Scripture quotations marked NASB are taken from the (NASB®) New American Standard Bible®, Copyright © 1960, 1971, 1977, 1995, 2020 by The Lockman Foundation. Used by permission. All rights reserved. www.lockman.org

Scripture quotations marked WNT are taken from the NEW TESTAMENT IN MODERN SPEECH by Richard Francis Weymouth, published in 1903; public domain

Hardcover ISBN: 979-8-9870188-0-4

Paperback ISBN: 979-8-9870188-1-1

eBook ISBN: 979-8-9870188-2-8

Published by Ready Writer Press

Printed in the USA by Palmetto Publishing

Cover design by Ivan Kurylenko

Author headshot by Morgan Crouch

Editing by Anne Balke

Visit the author's website at www.carastarns.com

Acknowledgements

Where would I be without Jesus?

Lord, You're my best friend, my beloved, my everything.

Only You know what it took to redeem me.

Thank You for everything. I love You.

Sincerely, Your friend

To my leaders who guard me and guide me, thank you.

To my brothers and sisters in Christ who always strengthen and encourage me, thank you.

To my family, thank you for your incredible support. I love you.

A few more. Steve and Mary Rife, Pastor Tim Jones, and Rhea Zigmund.

I feel like I've lived a million lifetimes already, and I wanted to quit at every turn of the corner. Thank you for the open arms to cry, to be instructed, encouraged, and known.

You shaped this book into what it is. But you also shaped me into who I am.

Lord, thank You for training my hands for battle.

(Psalm 18:34)

"I pursued my enemies and overtook them;

I did not turn back till they were destroyed.

I crushed them so that they could not rise;

they fell beneath my feet."

Psalm 18:37–38 (NLT)

"The Lord is my light and my salvation;

Whom shall I fear?

The Lord is the stronghold of my life;

Of whom shall I be afraid?"

Psalm 27:1

Table of Contents

Prologue   1

The Overcomer's Field Guide   5

Introduction   9

1. Weapons for What?   19
2. The Foothold   28
3. The Snowball Effect   44
4. Starting Line: Love and Power   63
5. Deliverance is a Miracle   86
6. Surprising Obstacles   116
7. The Shotgun Sniper   129
8. Unsheathe the Sword   136
9. The Perfect Sacrifice   151
10. The Battering Ram   184
11. Prayer Tactics for Whoopin'   209
12. The Power of a Plan   243
13. Dealing with Return Visitors   252
14. Roll Call   259

Appendix   271

About the Author   295

References   296

Prologue

Dear overcomer, don't use the Bible as a crutch to comfort you, when it's meant to be a weapon to deliver you.

I want to give a spoiler upfront because it pertains to the believer.

First, allow me to preface the statement by giving some context to my faith journey over the years. I remember talking to Jesus as a little girl. I loved Him deeply even at a young age. I was raised in the church and abided closely in friendship with the Holy Spirit. I studied the Word and discipled many others. Maturing into high-school, my church began to stir up the call of ministry and leadership over my life. They equipped me by giving me positions on committees and a voice in church matters. Right after college, they confidently sent me overseas on my own. I raised up a successful ministry in Uganda, trained the local church to lead it, and came home one year later. Shortly after, God opened up a door for me to work in a ministry that supports trafficked women through healing and recovery. After three years growing in leadership there, God called me to launch a nonprofit to help trafficked youth.

Throughout all this time, God did many miracles in my life, grounded me firmly in scripture, and His Spirit encountered me powerfully in prayer. My spiritual resume was stacked. But what happened throughout much of that time may come as a surprise to you. I assure you; it came as a surprise to me.

You'll soon find out that as a spirit-filled Christian I was somehow tormented by spiritual warfare for six years. Before I lose too many readers on that statement, let's define spiritual warfare by using scripture. The Bible teaches us that believers are in a spiritual battle:

> *For our struggle is not against flesh and blood, but against the rulers, against the authorities, against the powers of this dark world and against the spiritual forces of evil in the heavenly realms. (Ephesians 6:12)*

> *For though we walk in the flesh, we are not waging war according to the flesh. For the weapons of our warfare are not of the flesh but have divine power to destroy strongholds. (2 Corinthians 10:3–4 ESV)*

> *Be alert and of sober mind. Your enemy the devil prowls around like a roaring lion looking for someone to devour. (1 Peter 5:8)*

Spiritual warfare, according to scripture, is when a believer is targeted and afflicted by the Devil and battling against supernatural forces. I won't spoil too much else, but growing up in the conservative Methodist church, it's safe to say I was *shocked* when I encountered a demonic spirit. Suddenly, those scriptures didn't seem so metaphorical after all!

My experience was never over-exaggerated because my instinct was to minimize and ignore the matter. I tried that for six years and it didn't work. Actually, things got worse. I found out that if a Christian allows the Devil to take a foothold, it can quickly evolve into a stronghold. I was a Jesus lover who studied the scriptures, served in the church, and walked closely with the Holy Spirit to hear His voice and witness miracles unfold before my very own eyes. The question then becomes; If I was a solid believer and faithful follower, how was the Devil able to torment me?

Because I used scripture as a crutch instead of as a weapon.

I was twenty-three years old when this battle began. As a young adult fresh out of college and a traumatic experience, I had a few "open doors" to close. After taking care of those matters, the affliction and torment still remained. It took me six years to figure out why. It's because as a believer, I was indoctrinated by Western Christianity to ignore spiritual warfare and use scripture as a crutch instead of as a weapon. (Why would I need a weapon if spiritual warfare didn't exist?) I consoled myself with scriptures of peace, comfort, love, grace, and the proverbial "thorn in the flesh" that makes my weakness a vessel for God's power! My goodness. No wonder the Devil could walk all over me. I was a pushover who used the Bible to comfort me when I needed it to deliver me.

I give this spoiler in advance so that I can help believers who've been afflicted by the Devil and can't seem to pinpoint how or why. First, I want to invite you to accept the reality of spiritual warfare as it is taught in scripture—the Devil targets believers, but if we defend ourselves, we overcome spiritual battles. Second, I invite you to use your biblical weapons of warfare for their express purpose: *Warfare*. Dear overcomer, don't use the Bible as a crutch to comfort you, when it's meant to be a weapon to deliver you.

The Overcomer's Field Guide

In military terms, a stronghold is set up for one of two reasons, and that's to either protect a land or overtake it. For protective purposes, a stronghold acts as a fortress to defend a city against attack. On the other hand, an encroaching enemy will build a stronghold in a territory it intends to overtake. In the case of the enemy camp, the stronghold serves as a base of operations from which the enemy advances its presence and mission to seize and destroy the city.

We see in the Bible that godly and ungodly strongholds are mentioned. Psalm 27:1 says, "The Lord is the stronghold of my life; Of whom shall I be afraid?" Psalm 18:2 and 94:22 also write about God being a stronghold to the believer, while 2 Corinthians 10:4–6 speaks about strongholds that are set up against God and the believer. You can be certain that when the enemy sets up a stronghold in your life, it is to crush you, overtake you, and stop you from fulfilling God's plans for your life. When this happens, you can either be a pushover, or you can *defend yourself.*

DEFEND YOURSELF

"Defend Yourself" is not an ordinary study experience, it is a tactical playbook. These pages are designed to equip the believer to use biblical strategies of militant proportions to overcome the enemy. That being said, you'll want to know where you're headed. At the end of every chapter, you will find a *Tactical Training*. In these trainings, you will *"drill in"* core truths, *"drill out"* strategic exercises, and *"drill down"* key scriptures. These exercises will introduce you to your weapons of warfare and get you practicing the strategies as they are taught. Finally, at the end of the book, you will find a *worksheet*. This is where it all comes together—the big *boom*. After having studied biblical strategies and putting them into practice, you'll be ready to execute a spiritual action plan to finally destroy those strongholds and enforce your victory in Christ! That's your field guide. The teachings equip you; the drills train you; and the worksheet activates you.

How you approach the reading experience, though, can be done in a few ways. This book is scripture heavy. This is very important because the journey concludes in a spiritual action plan in which you'll be using scripture as your ammo to defeat the lies of the Devil. Some of you may want to stop and look up scriptures as you read (like a Bible study); however, for others this may distract you from the lesson as a whole. To make the process easier for you, the scriptures used in each chapter are provided in the *Tactical Training* pages that follow the chapter.

If you "drill down" these scriptures, you'll have already done your homework before you even get to the end of the book! You can drill down scriptures by looking them up and meditating on them, or by memorizing the ones that speak to your circumstances. I encourage you to have your Bible next to you as you read through the *Tactical Training* pages so that you can switch directly over to scripture for further study.

You can use this book individually or walk through it with a group of friends. You can read the book straight through and circle back to the ***Tactical Trainings*** later, or you can pace yourself and do the drills as they come up. My recommendation? Consult the Holy Spirit each step of the way.

Remember, you are an overcomer (Revelation 12:11, Romans 8:37).

It's time to overcome!

Introduction

"I don't know where to look!", I cried out to God in distress. The attacks were coming from all directions, and they were overwhelming. I didn't know where to look, what to focus on first, or where to aim. Approaching this battle in the spirit looked pretty much like me swinging *blindly* at a piñata that kept dodging me, circling around, and then smacking me from behind. The Devil must have had a good laugh during that time, because even I knew I looked like a dummy.

I'll lead in by saying I don't attribute most problems in my life to the Devil. I've never been that person to name the Devil and his cohorts as the source to every issue. Sometimes the source is just the rough patches of life, oftentimes it's actually the fallout of my own flesh, and other times it's the consequences of my ignorance or sin. There are many reasons we might have problems and battles, and not all of them are arrows from the pit of hell. What I'm talking about, though, was *seriously* spiritual. There was a period of six years where the Devil had a true stronghold of torment over my life. It was so bad that I felt like I was dying, and when I didn't die, I wish I had. (I warned you; it was bad!) Coming from a conservative Methodist background, I had no vocabulary to wrap around what was happening without sounding crazy or alarming the buttoned-up Christians in my life.

It all started with Post Traumatic Stress Disorder (PTSD) from a car accident while I was overseas. An armored truck speeding in a military convoy hit my vehicle and I was shoved off the highway. I was sent plummeting downhill at an angle, making it a miracle that the car didn't flip. A scarier thought is that if it had, I might have flown out the windshield and been run over. During the course of the descent, I was tossed around like a rag doll because I had been on the passenger side resting fully reclined, rendering my seatbelt utterly useless. The Devil intended to kill me, but by the hand of God, I walked away from the accident.

After the accident, I was crippled by PTSD and bitterness toward God (Why didn't He just prevent the accident in the first place?). While the accident and subsequent PTSD were unfair, I had no clue that my bitterness toward God could give the Devil a foothold to afflict torment in my life (more on this later). This foothold evolved into a *literal chokehold.* One of the most terrifying torments I experienced was an unexplainable sensation of choking. Other torments included insomnia, depression, anger, worry, anxiety, constricted breathing, tormenting thoughts, voices in my head, and horrifying panic attacks. These torments nearly ruined my life, and they wanted to take my life.

Three years into this experience, the Lord healed me of the panic attacks in a supernatural manner. In one instant, my last panic attack was crushed to the ground and I've never had one since. Hallelujah! This supernatural deliverance ushered in an immense amount of relief. While this miracle took off more than half the pressure that was upon me, it wasn't the only torment in my life. With the panic attacks supernaturally lifted, this breathing room should have prompted me to focus on overcoming all the other torments that remained. But instead of using this relief as a chance to take care of the remaining footholds, I became so distracted by the mounting challenges in my life and the speed at which everything was moving that I became a sitting duck on the frontline.

So exactly what was going on during all those years? A lot. I was leading intense frontline ministry, confronted by spiritual warfare, with no spiritual awareness, and an overwhelming amount of trauma—all at a young age. (Sounds like a recipe for disaster to me.) While God's hand was undoubtedly guiding and sustaining me as my life moved at warp speed, I was left with no energy to deal with the torments that were trying to wipe me out. I just lived from hour to hour, and day to day hoping the enemy would eventually leave me alone. Since I didn't know how to fight the enemy, I became passive and neglectful. Simply put, I was a pushover and a punching bag for the Devil.

While the panic attacks never returned, the other torments drastically worsened as I walked deeper into my calling. When I launched Safe Passage and God removed the panic attacks, a new torment took the main stage. I began to experience something unexplainable. I started to choke for no reason. I struggled to eat, and I even struggled to drink water. I was short of breath, as if something was wrapped around my neck and chest, squeezing me, and I struggled to speak as my throat closed in on itself. It was absolute insanity. I was so embarrassed about the experience that I kept this information to myself. I was just so tired that when the torment wasn't happening, I swept the oppression under the rug and tried to forget about it. I simply tried to enjoy the days and moments I wasn't under duress. I even taught myself to *forget* about the torment. That's the only way I found to cope. When I had a moment of intermission from the torments, I trained myself to forget. In doing this, I put myself into a place of total delusion by trying to live a free life in between enslaved episodes. This was a big mistake.

I ignored a small, manageable flame, and that flame turned into a fire that became so out of control it was almost unmanageable to contain and unfathomable to put out. I should have tackled the small fire when I had the window to do so when it was a reasonable size, but instead, I had to deal with an out-of-control wildfire years later. If you act like a pushover, the enemy will seize the opportunity to take more shots—because when you give the Devil one foothold, one single foothold, it doesn't matter how small it is, he now has a hold on you and he will always want more. *Give him an inch and he will take a mile!*

> *I put myself into a place of total delusion by trying to live a free life in between enslaved episodes.*

Finally, nearly six years into this I experienced something bizarre. Bizarre turned into harrowing. One day I heard a voice that wasn't mine. Against my better judgment, I ignored it because of the overload in my life. I was inundated with so many other challenges that demanded my immediate attention, so I just ignored this thing. I ignored it when it showed up and I ignored it when it spoke. (I'm telling you. When you let the enemy take an inch, it's not long before he claims the rest.)

After ignoring this awful, antagonizing voice for about nine months, it finally appeared visibly. It was an unsettling experience as I came face-to-face with something my mental health background and conservative Christian background had never prepared me for. When a vile form of darkness amassed in front of me in broad daylight, I realized the voice that had been tormenting me was a demonic spirit. I could not believe it, but that didn't matter, because the assault was real, terrifying, and serious. I had a demonic assailant on my hands and I didn't have a choice to not believe it. It attacked me and left me dizzy before I could even mutter the words, "Did that really just happen?". It was a mind tormenting spirit that terrified, silenced, and paralyzed me in the matter of *milliseconds*.

Suddenly, I could hardly hear, see, think, or speak through the dense presence of this demonic spirit. It was like trying to talk over something screaming in my face, wincing to see past a mountain of smoke, and struggling to hear through muffled waters. It was more than I could bear. Desperate, I rushed into a prayer center for help. *I had never met these prayer ladies in my life.* Feeling low-key "crazy" about hearing and seeing a demonic spirit, I didn't tell the minister anything when I walked in. I simply asked her to pray for me. The minister took a few minutes to pray in the spirit, then with a word of knowledge (1 Corinthians 12:8), she said to me, *"I see a cage over your mind, and I see trauma from Uganda."*

Here I was, finally battling psychotic torment in my mind because of the footholds from a car accident six years prior. All those years of being a spiritual couch potato, never putting out the fires, I became the ultimate pushover and punching bag. I passively allowed the Devil to take more and more until I had to check myself into a prayer center for hearing and seeing spirits.

At this point, my freedom became a matter of great urgency. I did not know what else would occur if I didn't get rid of this horrid spirit, and *soon*. Not knowing much about spiritual warfare, it became obvious to me that I had to clear out every last foothold in my life. Not even one could remain standing, or the Devil would find collateral to begin the siege all over again.

I was *terrified* to leave the prayer team's couch. I didn't want to be left alone, under the strong-arm of this assailant. Nevertheless, the time came for me to go home. I dusted myself off and I approached the throne room of Heaven with my Bible in hand. I knew my Bible held an armory of weapons and I just needed to load the ammo, but I was a novice. I didn't know where to start, I didn't know what weapons to use, nor how to fire them. I was fighting multiple battles against my own flesh and against the enemy, let alone the battles that come with running a frontline ministry in the fight against child trafficking.

I was overwhelmed and I felt ambushed. I cried out to God, "I don't know where to start, and I don't know where to look!"

He is so faithful. He showed me biblical tactics that combine faith, power, authority, and persistence. (Read that one more time.) Consider the difference between a handgun and shotgun. While a traditional handgun fires a single bullet, shotgun shells use a capsule packed with numerous lead pellets. When the capsule is launched into the air, these pellets explode like fireworks. Although this makes a shotgun ideal for chasing down a moving target, it lacks lethal accuracy against a swarm of enemies. You might get lucky and take out one target, but not the whole lot.

The Holy Spirit began to speak to me about a combo weapon that can destroy numerous enemies and strongholds at once, and with lethal accuracy. This is a biblically designed weapon. I call it the Shotgun Sniper. What is it? It's all of our weapons of warfare (2 Corinthians 10:4) loaded and fired at once—making one big *BOOM!* Together, the ammo blasts in all directions like a powerful shotgun and hits every bullseye with the accuracy of a sniper. It's the perfect weapon for desperate people who need a victory, and fast. Lives are hanging in the balance, just as mine was. I dug my heels into the ground, and I told God, "I'm going to use this strategy every day until this thing breaks, even if it takes the rest of my life." Using this gung-ho approach, it took me *two weeks* to break a *six-year* cycle.

I'll say that one more time. I lived in spiritual oppression and torment for six years. For six years the enemy ran me into the ground, choked me, strangled me, tormented me, intimidated me, and tried to take my life. I lived overwhelmed, hopeless, and oppressed for six years. Once I got tactical, it took two weeks to break every stronghold!

Whether you are dealing with a strong and stubborn flesh that won't yield and needs to be crucified through more drastic efforts (stop asking, and stop treating your flesh nicely!), or whether you're dealing with vile spiritual attacks, I want to show you how God empowered me to use biblical ammo and authority to win back my life in the matter of two weeks! Jesus didn't die for us to be pushovers. He didn't die for a freed people to settle back into slavery and oppression. It's time you stand up and defend yourself. The Devil's heard it before, but he's gotta hear it from *your* mouth. Go on. Tell it to him! *"Away from me, Satan!"*

TACTICAL TRAINING

Drill In

Read: 2 Corinthians 10:3–6

Reflect: While the armor of God equips us with pieces for offense and defense, it's our weapons of warfare that provide a means for demolition and arrest.

What weapons of warfare are you familiar with? Can you think of a time that your biblical weapons helped you to defend yourself and overcome the enemy?

Drill Out

Let's get our hearts set on freedom. Pray this prayer, or one in your own words.

> *Holy Spirit, thank You for speaking to me and instructing me in all matters. Thank You that I'm a child of God, and You've equipped me to be an overcomer (Revelation 12:11, Romans 8:37). Lord, I invite You to teach me as I read on. Teach me things I didn't know about my biblical weapons of warfare. Instruct me, Lord, about strongholds in my life and how to tear them down. Open my eyes to my authority in Christ, and help me to walk in total freedom, just as Your Word proclaims, "So if the Son sets you free, you will be free indeed." (John 8:36)*

Drill Down

1 Corinthians 12:8

Ephesians 6:12

1 Peter 5:8–9

John 3:16–20

CHAPTER 1

Weapons for What?

Fencing is a highly skilled sport based on the art of sword fighting. Fencing demands speed and accuracy, the ability to anticipate, quick reflexes, and great mental strength. (These are areas that we could all improve on when it comes to our own spiritual sword fighting.) The combative sport is known for its famous signal in which the opponent shouts, "En guarde!". The French word means "on guard", or to be on your guard. An athlete yells, "En guarde!" as a warning. It's a call to the fencer to adopt a defensive stance in readiness for an attack. In other words, the player demands, "Defend yourself!". Unfortunately for us, the enemy gives no such warning.

As in any sport, a serious athlete will spend time studying their opponent. Going into a match without knowing anything about your opponent is unwise. Many athletes actually watch their opponent's performance in other matches so as to study them. Before facing off, the athlete wants to know how tall their opponent is, how fast they are, what their signature moves are, what their strengths and weaknesses are, who they have defeated before, and all things about their nature and abilities. The Bible acts as our coach, playing the tape to tell us who the Devil is, what his signature moves are, and how we can overcome him. The Devil won't call out, "En guarde!" as a favor to us, but the Bible sure does. The Bible announces the enemy as a predator. Satan lures, he preys, he crouches and waits to pounce and devour you. In 1 Peter 5:8 Peter warned, "Be alert and of sober mind. Your enemy the Devil prowls around like a roaring lion looking for someone to devour." In John 10:10 Jesus said the enemy is a thief who comes to steal, kill, and destroy.

With such an atrocious enemy on the loose, did our Lord and Savior leave us defenseless against our foe? Not a chance! Like a good coach and trainer, Christ has fully equipped us to stand against the Devil's schemes. So why do we have a bunch of Christian pushovers? One issue is that there is little teaching about spiritual warfare and many Christians today are not walking in the fullness that God intended for us. Dr. Tony Evans, founder, and senior pastor of Oak Cliff Bible Fellowship in Dallas, puts it this way, "There is a lack of understanding about the spiritual realm and the influence that it has on the physical realm. The spiritual precedes, influences and, to many degrees, determines the physical realm. The better we understand the spiritual and how it relates to the physical, the better we are able to operate as Christians."[1] Unfortunately, many Christians literally don't believe that spiritual warfare actually imposes on our physical reality. Some don't believe a Christian can be attacked, tormented, or demonized and they absolutely won't have anything to do with the topic. This has left so

---

1   Evans, Tony. As stated in an interview with Jim Daily for *Decision* magazine. *The Reality of Spiritual Warfare: A Conversation With Tony Evans* (January 24, 2005), https://decisionmagazine.com/the-reality-of-spiritual-warfare.

many of God's people in a vulnerable position where they've actually let down their guard and become all the more vulnerable.

Isaiah 54 tells us that God's servants have a certain heritage and vindication from the Lord. Here's what this verse claims our heritage to be, it says, "No weapon formed against you shall prosper…" (Isaiah 54:17 [NKJV]). This is our inheritance and vindication, something to celebrate, yet since so many people have misunderstood the verse, they become disheartened in hardship. We see this happen when an arrow of hardship hits a person, and their reaction is to question this verse—doubting God's Word, power, faithfulness, truthfulness, fatherliness, and supremacy over evil. A person might spend their whole life stuck in bitterness toward God, hurt that a good God would allow something bad to happen to them. We get to this lifeless and loveless place when we misinterpret the scripture through a lens of self-preservation, and then use our bad experiences as a water-tight argument against the existence of a good God.

People mistake this verse to mean that no weapon will be *formed* against them, which is not true at all. This misleading expectation is the source of so much anger and bitterness that hurt people have against God. When something harms them, they turn on God because they believe either He isn't real like they thought, or He's real but not good. Such a small (yet critical) scriptural misunderstanding has disappointed the faith of many. God does not baby-proof us from evil, He *delivers* us from evil!

In Psalm 18, the psalmist writes that the Lord is his rock, fortress, deliverer, refuge, shield, the horn of his salvation, and his stronghold. How does he know the Lord is his deliverer? Because God *delivered* him. To state the obvious, there must have been a need to deliver him. In Psalm 18:4–5, David describes exactly what kind of attack he experienced, he explains, "The cords of death entangled me; the torrents of destruction overwhelmed me. The cords of the grave coiled around me; the snares of death confronted me." This is no small-scale attack, the man has come face to face with death and destruction. The Lord delivered him because he was under attack. In other words, weapons were formed. This man was entangled, overwhelmed, and confronted by these formations.

> *God does not baby-proof us from evil, He delivers us from evil!*

If the forerunners in the Bible misinterpreted Isaiah 54:17 to mean no weapon would be *formed* against them, they would have been extremely surprised when they were enslaved, attacked on all sides, thrown into a fire, into a lion's den, stoned to death, shipwrecked, beheaded, flogged, run out of town, exiled, imprisoned, crucified, and more than we know! If the main players in the Bible had mistaken Isaiah 54:17 to mean weapons would not be formed against them, their faith would have died in the face of their first trial. And yet Paul explained that he actually had *joy* in the midst of suffering! How can this be? Because we can take great confidence that the weapons that are formed against us *shall not prosper* (Isaiah 54:17).

Paul had great confidence in the middle of his suffering because he knew it was going to advance the gospel and establish God's kingdom all the more. The enemy comes to steal, kill, and destroy. He hopes to prosper *his* efforts. Weapons will be formed, but when we are yielded to God, the enemy's efforts will never prosper. When the Christians were persecuted, martyred, and displaced across the world, the enemy hoped to quench the movement. Instead, he fanned the flame. Those believers took refuge in other lands and thereby advanced the gospel far across the globe! We have our faith today *because* of the weapons that formed against the early church. The weapons formed, but they did not prosper for anyone except the Lord.

Paul realized the battle at hand was serious business. Thus, he found it important to write a letter to the church about the armor of God (See Ephesians 6. We'll cover this topic more in later chapters.) Why would Paul write about armor? It wasn't a figurative letter; it was for practical reasons only; *we are in a battle and we need defense.* He explains that the battle is not against flesh and blood, it's actually a spiritual battle in which we are dealing with rulers, authorities, powers of this dark world, and spiritual forces of evil in the heavenly realms (Ephesians 6:12). The foes he mentions are *very* specific. He actually classifies ruling spirits who are assigned to different territories, realms, and levels of authority. If it hasn't dawned on you yet, we are up against these very forces. Some are high, some are low, some are working in this world, and some are working in the heavenlies. Paul is presenting a spiritual battle against supernatural forces, and he arms us accordingly with spiritual equipment! We have spiritual defenses because we are in a spiritual battle.

This I propose to you. We are not defenseless in this battle; therefore we should defend ourselves. In Ephesians 6:11 Paul doesn't say to put on this armor so you can look good in uniform. You have armor so you can stand firm against the Devil's schemes. In other words, Paul is saying, "Defend yourself!"

2 Corinthians 10 speaks of warfare. It says, "For the weapons of our warfare are not carnal, but mighty through God to the pulling down

of strongholds; Casting down imaginations, and every high thing that exalts itself against the knowledge of God, and bringing into captivity every thought to the obedience of Christ." (2 Corinthians 10:4–6 [KJV]). This verse has a *militant* theme. Our weapons of warfare actually drive us to pull down, cast down, and bring opposition into captivity. While the armor of God equips us with pieces for offense and defense, it's our weapons of warfare that provide a means for demolition and arrest. If this is what we have been equipped with, one should assume we'll actually need the equipment. The very reason we have weapons of warfare is to defend ourselves and annihilate the enemy.

> **We are not defenseless in this battle; therefore, we should defend ourselves.**

Experiencing warfare doesn't mean God has let us down. God allows us the privilege to defend ourselves because we are not defenseless, and He wants us to operate in our authority. In Luke 22:31–32 Jesus told Simon Peter that the Devil wanted to "sift" the disciples, "Simon, Simon, Satan has asked to sift all of you as wheat. But I have prayed for you, Simon, that your faith may not fail. And when you have turned back, strengthen your brothers." When Satan came to sift Peter, Jesus didn't prohibit Satan, nor did he spare Peter from the fight. Instead, He *prayed* for Peter. Jesus also wasn't blindsided when the enemy came to sift Peter because Jesus knows Satan's signature moves. Every beast has a signature move. No one is surprised when a lion devours a gazelle or when a whale slurps up a school of fish. No one is surprised when a creature acts in its nature by attacking with its signature move. Nor was Christ surprised when the predator came to prey. Notice that Jesus didn't step in and take over for Peter. *When the Devil preys, Jesus prays.* Why does He allow the enemy to try and sift us? Because Christ knows what's in our nature—*and it's Him!* Through Christ in us, we have been given authority to overcome *all* the power of the enemy, and we are more than conquerors (Romans 8:37). Luke 10:19 states that we *can* overcome the enemy, and Revelation 12:11 prophecies *we will.* When the enemy came to sift Peter, Jesus didn't run interference, instead He encouraged Peter to *defend himself.* So it's time for you to do what a conqueror would do. Defend yourself!

TACTICAL TRAINING

Drill In

Read: Ephesians 6:10–17

Reflect: Paul is presenting a battle against supernatural forces, and he arms us accordingly with spiritual equipment! To state the obvious: we have spiritual defenses because we are in a spiritual battle.

Read: John 10:10

Reflect: Jesus said the enemy comes to steal, kill, and destroy. Do you feel like you've been spiritually alert and overcoming of the enemy's schemes, or have you been taught to ignore the enemy and discount spiritual warfare in your life?

Read: Ephesians 6:18

Reflect: Paul says that we should pray in the Spirit on all occasions and with all types of prayers and requests. He likens prayer to alertness. If we do not have a prayer life, how does this impact our spiritual alertness?

Drill Out

Consider (and perhaps revisit) what happened when the Israelites were cornered at the Red Sea, when they overtook the walls of Jericho, and when Gideon overcame the Midianites with only three hundred men (Exodus 14:1–31, Joshua 6:1–27, Judges 7:1–25).

In each case, God gave His people special instructions pertaining to the specific battle at hand, and they were victorious. For our next drill, you will go to the Lord in prayer and ask Him to give you a sober and alert mind for the battle ahead, and to speak to you about your specific circumstances.

Pray this prayer, or one in your own words.

I am spiritually sober and alert (1 Peter 5:8, Ephesians 6:18). I call my mind, soul and spirit to be spiritually discerning under the authority of Jesus Christ and the leading of the Holy Spirit. Holy Spirit, I ask You to reveal to me if anything going on in my life, past or present, is related to or impacted by spiritual warfare. (Pause and listen, then resume.) Lord, I ask You to reveal to me how You want me to defend myself and overcome the enemy's schemes and power. I know Your voice (John 10:27). I ask You to give me specific battle instructions by the leading of the Holy Spirit and in line with Your Word. Speak Lord, Your servant is listening (1 Samuel 3:10, Jeremiah 33:3).

Drill Down

Isaiah 54:17 **Luke 10:19**

Psalm 18:1-5 **Romans 8:37**

Luke 22:31–32 **Revelation 12:10–11**

CHAPTER 2

The Foothold

By the end of this book, you'll be equipped to demolish every stronghold and torment that has been ruining your life. But before we get to the explosives, we need to do a little "recon work". That's military code for surveying the situation. Many of us are in a mess because of *footholds*. The stronghold is the result, but the foothold is the source. When 2 Corinthians 10:3–5 speaks of strongholds, it speaks of tearing down thoughts, beliefs, and behaviors that are against God. These are the footholds that the enemy grabs for, and overtime, they become the foundation, cornerstones, and building blocks to set up strongholds. Before we get to destroying strongholds, we have to remove every last foothold that might sabotage our mission. When it comes to tearing down strongholds, you stand a better chance at completing the mission when you destroy every last foothold. Trust me, you don't want to start this and quit halfway through.

Strongholds and footholds work together, and the infestation is something to the effect of bed bugs. If you spend hundreds of dollars bug-bombing your home and you let your favorite sweater skip the bonfire, you'll see another infestation in less than a week's time and you'll be starting the toilsome process all over again. It's the same with strongholds and footholds. If you spend all your time and energy tearing down a stronghold but you spare a foothold because you are blind to it or have an attachment to it, you'll be back in the fight in a matter of no time. Jennifer and Ron Eivaz, senior pastors of Harvest Church, have a saying that goes like this, "Whatever you don't deal with, will deal with you. It will choose the time and place, and it will cost you more." Gill Finley, pastor of Heavenly Outpour Church, says, "If you don't give it over, it will be the very thing Satan tries to come for later."[2] Extermination is not something you want to start over on! You will want to do this in one thorough, clean sweep so you can quit wasting time and energy being pummeled into the ground and finally strike a blow that's going to put you in charge.

> *The stronghold is the result, but the foothold is the source.*

I want to show you from my own story how one foothold snowballed into numerous others, and how this gave way for the enemy to erect powerful strongholds in my life. In the end, I had an infestation on my hands. I debated long and hard about sharing my experience with the world. I've decided to go into great detail about my story, and I want you to know why. I could teach about the danger of footholds without

---

2 Finley, Gill, personal communication, paraphrased and used with permission.

using my testimony, but my experience proves to what extent a foothold can sabotage a person's life. My story is a clear example of how the Devil gets from point A to point B—from foothold to stronghold. I want to expose the enemy and fortify the believer.

BACK TO THE BEGINNING

In 2014, I was working in Uganda as a missionary for the United Methodist Church. It was a brutal year. At the time, Uganda was among the most corrupt nations in the world. I could see this at the micro and macro levels—from simply being cheated on the price of an avocado to being turned away by the visa agent unless I agreed to a "dinner date". Yikes. The daily frustrations were enough to deal with, but I was soon faced with much worse. The region was still recovering from a heinous war that had occurred decades prior. Witchcraft, violence, crime, and evil were still wreaking havoc everywhere. During my year there, I witnessed just a small sampling of the awful things that were happening within the country. One of the local nonprofits had a revolt among the workers where they tried to stone the missionaries. Another missionary had her home broken into in the middle of the night. She was violently stabbed and had to be flown to a hospital. One person was murdered and another poisoned in the local network of our quaint town. Finally, my closest friend died a horrific death, due to a terrible asthma attack triggered by the dusty climate. Among other things I don't feel I should mention, it was an unimaginably challenging year.

I was already dealing with grief, burnout, and extreme distrust when the Lord spoke to me one day. For once, I was enjoying a beautiful afternoon. I was turning a corner and healing from the loss of my friend, and my joy was slowly returning. I remember the day with great detail.

I was cruising down the desert road in my epic RAV4. The windows were down and the dust that kicked up applied a heavy coating to my hair and skin. The music was setting the most beautiful scene. I rolled down my window to feel the air, gritty with orange dust. Thrilled about the scenic road trip, I threw my arm out into the powdery wind and *smiled*. I remember taking a deep breath as I melted into the simplicity, dirtiness, awe, and wonder of that moment. Then in the quiet of the very moment, I heard the Lord speak. I heard Him clear as day. He surprised me by asking a strange question. He asked, *"If you got into a car accident, would you trust Me?"*

I ignored the question, attributing it to a wayward thought. But the question came again. It came softly, and with great peace. *"If you got into a car accident, would you trust Me?"* I said, "Lord, You can't be serious. If You know an accident is going to happen, why wouldn't You just stop it?" His reply came with the same question a third time. I wondered if this was a test like that of Abraham's test with Isaac (Genesis 22), measuring surrender. I assured myself that God would prevent such an incident, and that He must be merely assessing my trust. I replied, "Sure, Lord. I would trust You."

A month later I had completed my year-long commitment and it was time to go home. After a terribly traumatic year, I was happy to be headed to the airport. My Ugandan pastor came to escort me, and I buckled up for a seven hour trip, one I had taken many times before. As soon as we got on the road, though, something strange occurred. When we turned on the highway I was overcome with this eerie and looming feeling that we were going to be hit. When we turned onto the highway that stretched for seven hours straight, something in my spirit became highly aware of an oncoming collision. This was not paranoia, but a supernatural awareness. Suddenly, I remembered God's question to me a month before.

This might be a good time to point out that we don't get to choose how the supernatural moves in our lives. I can't change my experience; I can only attempt to explain it. If I was older and as experienced in the supernatural as I am now, who knows, maybe I would have commanded the accident to cease and be canceled. Yet I don't think so because the greater glory was in the outcome. When God's own instruction came to me a month before, He didn't instruct me to pray it off. He instructed me to *trust*. In fact, that's what I kept hearing on that seven-hour road trip; I kept hearing a fatherly voice that was calm, cool, and collected. As self-preservationists, we want God to act through *prevention*. But prevention doesn't prosper us in the way that intervention is able to because there are certain levels of faith that are only forged through fire. What I sensed was intervention, not prevention. I turned my ear to the Holy Spirit to be sure, and I kept hearing God present the same question over and over again, asking, *"Do you trust Me?"* Although I was nervous, I said, "Yes, Lord, I trust You." The Lord was speaking to me about trusting Him, and I made my choice.

> **When the enemy tries to harm us, he's working to wipe out the deliverers!**

Some people struggle with what happened next. To which I say, "That's okay, let's work through it." Because I struggled with it too! But I was immature in my faith, immature in my understanding of God as the supreme Almighty, and immature in understanding what trusting God looks like. Consider the militant attributes of the Lord; He rebukes those who hotly pursue you, He sends forth His love and faithfulness, and He is working out what the enemy meant as harm for your good (Psalm 57:3, Genesis 50:20). What do *those* verses indicate? They indicate that the enemy pursues you and forms weapons against you. But what is God's promise? That the formed weapon shall not *prosper*, and God has the power to take an attack that was meant to harm you and reverse it for your good and His glory! Even a car accident.

Why would He allow us to go through something harmful? We find our answer in Genesis 50:20, which reads, "You intended to harm me, but God intended it for good to accomplish what is now being done, the saving of many lives." When the enemy tries to harm us, he's working to wipe out the deliverers! The reason God allows us to go through trial is because *when we are delivered, we become deliverers!* (Joseph, Moses, Daniel, Jesus, etc.!) No one wants to endure the suffering. But when you become delivered, you can accomplish the good that God intends, which is "the saving of many lives". The delivered person becomes a deliverer. Today, I've been able to help people struggling with Post Traumatic Stress Disorder (PTSD), panic attacks, mental illness, and torment because God delivered me from the same harm! What the enemy intends to harm you with, God intends to use it to save many lives—first yours and then countless others! As a member of Jennifer Eivaz's mentorship group, I have heard her say many times, "Don't you dare quit! People you haven't met yet are depending on your healing story. There are people who will need to hear your testimony to come through theirs!"[3] Are you encouraged? Now that we worked through that, let's return to the scene of the accident.

> *When you become delivered, you can accomplish the good that God intends, which is the saving of many lives.*

The entire road trip was a nightmare. It stormed like a terrible tsunami for the first six hours! We dodged dangerous semis that weaved around dazed and confused farm animals who were fending for their lives in a real-life version of Frogger. We squinted our eyes through the rainy windshield as we tried our best to navigate the unpaved, pothole riddled highway, while semis zoomed past each other, tipping on their wheels and playing chicken as they charged head on toward our vehicle in a daring attempt to get ahead on the highway. Any of this madness was dangerous on a normal day, but in the midst of a torrential downpour, it was hell to watch as the rain pounded the windshield, making it unbearable to see past the thick sheet of water that pixelated our terrifying view. This was actually a trip I had fearlessly driven countless times before. This trip, though, was like none before.

I reclined my seat and laid back as the Lord continued to speak to me about trusting Him. I was so afraid I could hardly hold it togeth-

---

[3] Eivaz, Jennifer, paraphrased from an Excellence in the Supernatural Online Mentorship teaching and used with permission. Learn more about Jennifer Eivaz at https://www.jennifereivaz.com.

er. I began to count the minutes, and the minutes turned to hours. Six of those hours later, the storm finally ceased. We came upon clear skies and dry roads. When the clouds parted, so did my anxiety. As we closed in on the city, congestion caused the traffic to slow down to a more reasonable speed. We were twenty minutes and an easy ride from our hotel, when suddenly, a military convoy approached from behind. A line of army vehicles started forcing its way through the center of the tightly zipped traffic. One after another, they sped forward and cars had no other choice but to quickly move aside. My friend who was driving gave the convoy as much room as he could, but we were as far over as we could go. We held our breath at the edge of a steep hill. Just as the last truck was finally passing by, it clipped us.

Suddenly, I felt our vehicle turn off the highway and we were sent plunging down a steep hill full of work sites and piles of brick. It was already a bumpy ride down, but to make matters worse, my seat had been entirely reclined. I experienced extreme whiplash—being thrown all the way to the back of the fully reclined seat and thrust back into the air again and again. In the chaos, I muttered something through my gritted teeth, and I bit a hole through my tongue as I did. (Turn that into a sermon.) I muttered, "Jeeesssuuusss." The mutter was a 50% plea to rescue me, and another 50% was attributed to the tune of bitter resentment. I wondered why God let this happen. I felt abandoned and forsaken. I was already mad at God and we hadn't even landed yet! At that point, all I could see was a green and blurry windshield as branches were being kicked up and tossed all around us. Finally, we came to a stop at the end of the hill. I tried to open my door and realized we landed in a bunch of bushes.

As I wedged myself out of that vehicle and inspected the scene, the truth is, I should have declared a miracle. We barreled down a hill *side-*

ways, over African shrubbery and piles of brick. *We should have flipped!* And had we flipped, my seatbelt would have done me no favors because my seat had been entirely reclined. I was tossed around like one of those floppy inflatable tube-men outside the car lots! I was jerked and thrown all over the place. If we had flipped, I would have been out the windshield, under the car, and probably dead. So when I inspected the scene, I should have inspected a bona fide miracle! *That's why God was telling me to trust Him!*

The enemy meant to harm me, but the Lord guided us down that hill to a very safe landing. It was traumatic, but it was honestly an incredible victory! I should have been praising God and giving Him glory because I walked away from an accident I could have died from! This was the problem with my attitude; when this event should have increased my trust in God, I turned on Him instead. I resented God *and I wanted Him to know it.* This was sheer rebellion on my part. I broke the pact I made to trust Him, even after having the life-sparing evidence that He could be trusted! Instead, I became angry, resentful, scared, and bitter. The orphan spirit in me came out, and it was ugly. What is an orphan spirit and how does it afflict the believer? It's a demonic plot to come against the spirit of adoption, making orphans out of heirs.

Romans 8:15 (AMP) says, "For you have not received a spirit of slavery leading again to fear [of God's judgment], but you have received the Spirit of adoption as sons [the Spirit producing sonship] by which we [joyfully] cry, 'Abba! Father!'" For so long, God's children lived in fear of His presence because of their sin and shame. But through the Holy Spirit, we receive the spirit of adoption and are invited to approach God with boldness and confidence (Hebrews 4:16)!

The enemy works in opposition to the spirit of adoption through an opposing orphan spirit. An orphan spirit is exactly what it sounds like, it is when a person feels or believes they are orphaned by God, usually due to painful experiences. An orphan spirit finds footholds on a person who has experienced traumatic detachment from a parent through loss, abandonment, or rejection. The orphan spirit had operated in my life since I lost my father to a heart attack when I was nine years old. When a child experiences any kind of trauma or abandonment, you might see their sadness, fear, and broken heartedness come through under the guise of anger.

Anger is often used as a wall to front a toughness when underneath, the person is actually feeling very broken, scared, and vulnerable. You see, for me, the one thing worse than losing a father is watching your loved ones lose their son, brother, friend, and husband. That was more difficult for me because not only did I carry my grief, but I carried our family's. Because I love my mother, I especially carried her grief, and this grief turned into a fear of loss. When I grew up, I had this resentment toward God about marriage. I began to twist God's arm. I would say things like, "Why should I get married when my husband might die?" This was the orphan spirit in operation.

You see, when a child is hurt, upset, and feels overlooked, abandoned, or forgotten, do they come to you and calmly ask for you to turn your caring attention to their needs? No. *They wail.* They scream at the top of their lungs. They cry crocodile tears. They make a big fuss, they pitch a fit, they pout *long* after the episode is over, and they twist your arm so that you will feel bad for them. A child can hardly look past a boo boo without blowing it all out of proportion. This is because when the child gets hurt, they feel vulnerable. They are so small and helpless that one little bump rattles them to their core. They make a big scene so that mommy and daddy will know they've been hurt. The parents are signaled to come running. The child exhibits these behaviors so that mom and dad will feel bad for them and do everything possible to make sure their baby never gets hurt ever again. At first this is just an instinctual pattern, but over time the child learns—sometimes subconsciously, sometimes consciously—that if they keep doing the same things, they can get the attention they so desperately want.

This is what I did to God Almighty. Whenever something bad happened in my life, the abandoned and brokenhearted child within emerged to try and make God feel bad for me, because maybe if I could make Him feel bad for me, He would make sure I never got hurt ever again.

When I pushed my way out of that car, I went into orphan mode. Although I knew deep in my spirit that I should have been rejoicing, I went to a place of resentment and bitterness. Instead of praising God for the incredible landing, I blamed Him for not stopping the accident in the first place. I twisted His arm for being a bad dad who overlooked His child getting hurt. So, for the next few weeks as I processed it all, I cried my crocodile tears. I pouted. I moped around. I pitched a fit and made a scene, and it was all an indecent and calculated effort to make God feel bad for me. I'm trying to tell you; I did this *knowingly*. A person who has an orphan spirit is dealing with insecurities of loss, danger, and abandonment. They can't just shed a tear and move on; they have to appeal to the emotions of their caretaker. Daddy softly saying, "You're okay, bud!", just won't do. The orphan has to tug on daddy's heartstrings. The orphan doesn't feel safe until daddy is on the ground, crying tears with baby, taking the blame, and saying, "I'm so sorry, I wasn't watching, this is all my fault. I'll never let it happen ever again, I promise."

> *A person who has an orphan spirit is dealing with insecurities of loss, danger, and abandonment. They can't just shed a tear and move on; they have to appeal to the emotions of their caretaker.*

That's what I wanted to hear from God—that He was sorry and that He would always keep me from getting hurt—but I never did. Even after the accident, all I ever heard Him speak about was trusting Him. As the following weeks passed by, it was very clear to me that He was giving me a grace period. He understood the scared little girl in me was triggered, and He was working tenderly to help me. I knew the Lord was working on me. I knew He was reaching out in His kindness to me. He wanted me back on the horse, and I wanted to hear Him promise me I'd never get bucked in life ever again. His offer kept coming to me, pleading, *"Trust me!"* I rejected this offer because I still hadn't heard the golden words I was waiting for, "I'll never let it happen ever again."

Let me assure a few people before we move forward; I knew I was in rebellion. I knew I was overreacting, and I knew I was blowing everything out of proportion in an attempt to manipulate God. I knew this even at the time. And to come clean further, I knew God was giving me time to work through my emotions, but I rejected this healing because I wasn't going to move on until He gave me a no-more-boo-boo's guarantee. So, with indecorous stubbornness, I rejected the best offer I could ever be given. To trust God. Somehow, I knew this grace and invitation was time sensitive, a matter of great urgency. Discerning all of this, I still hardened my heart through manipulative tactics from the orphan spirit. I was very aware that I had dragged out my anger far beyond its grace period, and this rebellion to not trust God was the worst mistake I ever made in my life. It created a monstrous foothold for the enemy that snowballed into six years of torment.

I want to point out that anger toward God is not initially rebellion. God understands our feelings and defenses, even our anger. He ministers to those places to heal us, free us, and prove His amazing love for us. It's not a sin to grieve, wail, and express your true and unadulterated feelings over your experiences. In reading the Bible, you will find many people who couldn't hold back from expressing their raw emotions. Job cursed the day he was born (Job 3:1). Moses complained about his job, telling God it was a trouble and burden to lead the Israelites (Numbers 11:11). Most heart wrenching of all, when Jesus was dying on the cross, He cried out, "My God, my God, why have you forsaken me?" (Matthew 27:46). All of these cries went straight to God's ears. When the Father hears our cry, He doesn't turn away from us, He turns to us. In Psalm 40:1, David says, "He turned to me and heard my cry."

He is our Father, Advocate, Comforter, Healer, and Deliverer. He is called Immanuel, which means, "God with us"! You are not the first person who has tried to hide from God. Someone who once tried eventually gave up and wrote, "Where can I go from your Spirit? Where can I flee from your presence? If I go up to the heavens, you are there; if I make my bed in the depths, you are there." (Psalm 139:7–8). No matter how deeply you've dug yourself into a trench of darkness, you cannot escape God. *He is there.* Some of us have befriended our darkness, but Psalm 139:11 says even the darkness cannot hide you because it's not dark to God. He sees you because He searches for you. That's how much He loves you. He shows up to minister to you even in your darkness, even when you've made your bed in the depths of despair. His name is *God with us.* He is near to the brokenhearted and saves those who are crushed in spirit (Psalm 34:18). Your anger is not sin, but Ephesians 4:26 points out that it's easy for us to sin in our anger. It is dangerous for us to hold onto anger when God works so tenderly to help and heal us so we can be free. Anger is one letter short from danger. If we hold onto our anger for too long, it becomes a danger to us.

Anger (toward anyone, but especially toward God) is a great danger because it can become a foothold *over time* when we refuse to allow God to minister to us. While God does not rush a broken heart, He *will* lead you to let go of the bitterness, rage, anger, and unforgiveness. These things cause a root (or foothold) to spring up and defile our lives, even defiling our communion with the Holy Spirit (Hebrews 12:15, Ephesians 4:30–31). Some of you have blocked God from ministering to your anger and this has caused numerous unclean roots to spring forth and defile your life. Others need to have peace that God is still ministering to your broken, but open, heart.

My story is only mine. Let the Holy Spirit bring peace and insight to where you are in yours. When it comes to my story, I knew I was fueling very small fears in an attempt to manipulate God. I was not ignorant at all, in fact, I was trying to strong-arm God into giving me control. Lastly, I knew I was running out of time. His hand of grace would not plead with me forever.

TACTICAL TRAINING

Drill In

Read: Genesis 50:20

Reflect: When the enemy tries to harm us, he's working to wipe out the deliverers. You can be sure that when God delivers you, you'll help Him deliver others.

Read: Deuteronomy 20:16–18, Judges 3:5–6

Reflect: God instructed the Israelites to clear the land. In other words: wipe out the enemy! When they stopped short, the pagan remnant infested Israel with sin, strife, and idolatry for hundreds of years. Have you experienced a similar effect in your life by letting footholds stick around?

Read: Ephesians 4:26–31

Reflect: Anger is one of the most destructive footholds the Devil can grab you by. Spend some time in prayer and ask the Holy Spirit if there is any anger in your heart that He wishes to free you from. Take your time, and include pastoral support as needed.

Drill Out

Time to do a little recon work. Let's survey the situation.

Q: Can you think of any issues that always seem to return, or things you can never defeat?

A:

Q: What are the reasons you allow certain ungodly remnants to remain in your life?

A:

Q: How would your life be different if you could finally be free?

A:

Drill Down

    Genesis 22

    Psalm 57:3

    Romans 8:15

    Psalm 139:7–11

    Psalm 34:18

    Ephesians 4:30–31

    Hebrews 12:15

CHAPTER 3

The Snowball Effect

I had moved back to the U.S. and was taking it easy as I settled back into life at home. As the weeks went by after the accident, I grew more and more hard-hearted against God. Although it was a total miracle that we were mostly unharmed in that accident, childhood fears resurfaced, and I became overwhelmingly afraid. Instead of using the event as an awesome reason to trust God, I used it as a bargaining chip. I bargained with God that I would trust Him if only He could promise I would never be hurt again.

The Lord wasn't looking at my calculated tactics or offended by my fierce anger. As my Father, He came near to me with His love. He persistently tried to minister to my heart, but instead of being vulnerable in those places, I became manipulative and rebellious, angrily pushing Him away lest He take my deal. It was "deal or no deal" for me. I wanted God's love, but I wanted it on my terms and conditions, because for an orphan spirit to re-enter into son or daughtership, they have conditions penned by trauma, loss, abandonment, fear, control, anger, and the need to dominate the outcome of the relationship. The enemy wants to use our childhood experiences to make us fear or despise a relationship with God, our true Father. (What a nefariously evil plan to make orphans out of sons and daughters!)

When God didn't take my deal on my terms, I tried to make Him feel my pain. So, I did the worst thing a child can do. When God loved me, I shoved it back. I rejected His love and would not receive it, reciprocate it, or dare to feel it. I did this because I knew I could hurt God's heart. All a good father wants is for his children to feel loved by him, so to be rejected by your own son or daughter is to grieve the loss of a child who never even died. I rejected God's love, hoping it would hurt Him more than me, and cause Him to change His mind about my deal.

Instead, He offered me a better deal—to surrender my life in exchange for perfect love without fear (1 John 4:18). Stubborn, I chose fear and rejected love. I wish I would have received His love, because I would have been healed of the present trauma along with my childhood trauma! Sometimes a trial in adulthood can become an opportunity to heal from something you weren't able to heal from in your childhood. Instead of being healed from two situations, we use the present to despise God all the more over our past.

When I made my bed in this type of deep-seated anger and turned my back on my Father's love, *things took a dim turn for the next six years of my life…*

THE FIRST ENCOUNTER

The Bible is not all that metaphorical about spiritual warfare.

A month after the accident, my whole life changed. What began as a boring afternoon escalated into a terrifying encounter I will never forget. I was laying on the couch when I saw something amass and come into view. Unbelief was quickly overridden by shock when I realized it was a spirit—something I had never seen before. It was formless, and it embodied utter darkness as a shadow. In a millisecond, it eclipsed over the air, the room, outside the window, inside the house—sweeping over everything like a curtain. Where there was light in my life for twenty-two years, suddenly a vile darkness came to tip the scales.

One minute I was watching TV, zoning out to Jeopardy, and the next, I felt like I was suddenly thrust into a re-enactment of Psalm 18:4–7. I was in a wrestling match. It felt as if the cords of death had wrapped around me, as if the snares of death had confronted me. Everything happened at once. The moment I saw the spirit, I thought I died. My heart *stopped*—then dropped—as I gasped for air. When I realized I wasn't dead, I was overcome by a feeling of doom—as if I had fallen into a hopeless pit of darkness. My head became heavy, and my entire mind was fuzzy and unclear. I could barely see, hear, or engage with my surroundings. I couldn't breathe; it was like I was forcing my lungs to stay alive. If you can imagine the muffled feeling of being submerged under water, that is how trapped I felt. I felt like I was drowning in my own body.

My doctor told me I experienced a panic attack, which is an unexplainable episode where you feel like you are dying. I didn't connect the dots until years later, but I'll connect them for you now. By the hand of God, I walked away from an accident that could have killed me. It didn't, because God was victorious. I should have walked away with a strengthened faith. Instead, I became paralyzed by fear.

Psalm 23:4 (KJV) says, "Yea, though I walk through the valley of the shadow of death, I will fear no evil: for thou art with me; thy rod and thy staff they comfort me." What I saw amass before me was the shadow of death that is mentioned in Psalm 23:4. The shadow of death is not metaphorical. Nor is the wrestling with evil spirits that Paul speaks of in Ephesians 6:12. The Bible is not all that metaphorical about spiritual warfare. I found this out the hard way, when I gave the enemy a foothold to wrestle me by. I rejected God's ministry to my heart and clung to my fear of death. If I wanted to fear death instead of trust God—the enemy could do something with that. And he did.

> ## *What I would not let go of was the very foothold Satan grabbed onto.*

The enemy doesn't play fair, especially not on childhood brokenness. He takes the open doors where he can, and he's not above being untasteful about it. Oh, how I should have accepted God's sweet invitation for comfort and freedom! The Lord tried so hard to help me, but I resisted. You can lead a horse to water, but you cannot make it drink. Finally, what I would not let go of was the very foothold Satan grabbed onto. The attack took less than one second to enter my life, and yet it had the power to ruin my life for the next six years. This is where it started. The demonic attack announced itself through a frightening encounter that knocked the breath out of me.

A SWEET AND SUPERNATURAL INTERLUDE

The torment happened in stages, and so did my deliverance. During the first three years I struggled with depression, PTSD, chronic insomnia, panic attacks, and sensations of choking, suffocating, and strangulation. I could barely drive. I struggled to do my job. I dreaded public speaking. Every panic attack made me feel like I was going to die, and when I didn't, the vicious cycle made me wish I had just so the terror would end. One day, I finally cried out to God, "I feel like I'm dying every single day, so why didn't you just do me a favor and kill me back there in the accident?!"

It was a long road. Finally, three years into this, the Lord delivered me from the heaviest part of the load. I had an important event coming up to launch my ministry, Safe Passage. I was nervous because not only was I supposed to stand in front of a crowd, but I would be standing behind the podium at the Governor's Mansion! I was terrified. Ever since my encounter with the evil spirit, anytime I spoke in a meeting or in front of a small group, I would have a panic attack and nearly faint. How was I supposed to stand in front of a crowd, let alone the governor?

This fear was so consuming it began to seep into my dreams. Many nights I woke up *gasping* for air. In the middle of the night, I would jolt awake from having a nightmare that I died in front of the governor because I couldn't breathe. This fear was so real to me because my dear friend Katie, the missionary in Uganda, died from asthma combined with a panic attack. My friend died the same way I felt like I was about to die every single day. This was an extremely distressing experience, and these nightmares were the final straw.

I contacted my doctor the next morning and asked if I could come in. I was already on medication for my panic attacks, but when the fear of death broke into my dreams, I emailed to ask if we could discuss something stronger—and soon. By the way, there is no shame in prescriptive medication! God works and heals through counseling, treatments, and medications. In fact, I tried several prescriptions and a number of treatment plans during those years with the support of my church, including their financial support. But a point came when I realized the medicine and counseling wasn't making a dent in my strongholds. I needed a spiritual breakthrough!

My doctor invited me to schedule an appointment so we could discuss options. I went online to complete the patient questionnaire when I heard the Lord speak to me. I stopped dead in my tracks, just short of submitting the appointment confirmation. God intercepted my determination and asked a question of His own. He asked, *"When I heal you, do you want to know beyond a shadow of a doubt that it was Me, and nothing else?"*

I slammed my laptop shut. I was one appointment away from getting stronger medication that could manage my problems. But for what I was dealing with, I knew complete freedom could only come from the power of God. Now I waited for a different kind of appointment.

The big event finally rolled around. I was a ball of nerves the entire day, wondering when the panic attack would hit, how bad it would be, and if I'd pass out in front of the governor like my nightmares foreshadowed. I hauled my box of supplies into the incredible mansion, and that's when the panic attack set in. My hands were shaking, my head felt like it was being pulled down by a 100-pound weight, a fog caused me to become clumsy, dizzy, and confused, and my heart raced. I felt like I was drowning, and I had no way out. I had one option only, so I put down the box and told myself, "Just set up in faith." I began to put out the brochures and prepared the event entirely in faith while this panic attack stole every breath I was trying to preserve for the speech.

Thirty minutes later I stopped dead in my tracks. I was involved with another task when I had this sudden feeling as if I had misplaced something significant. As I zigzagged through the corridors of this magnificent historical mansion that dated back more than two hundred years, I pondered in pure confusion. Then, as if something had just departed my soul, I gazed up at the twenty-foot ceilings in search of it. (I remember feeling surprised that I did this. Somehow, I knew in my spirit that something had left!) I looked to my side, and then behind me. *Something was missing,* yet in its void was the most tangible peace I had ever felt. I felt lighter. I felt free! Then it hit me, "IT'S GONE!"

It was like the story when Jesus healed ten men of leprosy, but they were healed as they went on their way (Luke 17:11–17). There had to be a moment on their walk to the temple when they thought, "Where did it go? It's gone! I can feel that it's gone! I can see that it's gone!" The Lord promised my deliverance, and He delivered me as I went forward in faith.

I was delivered from insomnia in a similar manner just months later.

Chronic insomnia disintegrates a person's emotional, physical and spiritual health. While a healthy person wakes up with renewed strength, a person with insomnia wakes up exhausted and defeated in body and soul. Spiritually, it causes a dark loneliness in the night hours that makes a person feel hopeless and godless. The enemy uses insomnia to prevent you from experiencing the peace and assurance of God's presence at night, which ultimately ends up dictating the rest of your day. Psalm 16:7–8 says that in the night, your heart should actually instruct you, reassuring you of His presence beside you.

One Sunday morning, I woke up depleted. This was about a year into chronic insomnia. At this point, I was sick in my body due to prolonged restlessness. I was also ridden with the angst that always carried over from a night of tossing, turning, and feeling hopelessly alone at a cosmic level. I forced myself to get dressed, got in the car with a lead foot, and drove to church. I was desperate for freedom. To my surprise, we had a guest speaker that day. I couldn't tell you what he preached on, because all I could think about was getting to the prayer team after the service. When that time came, I beat everyone to the front of the line and found myself standing before the guest speaker who knew nothing about me. With a prophetic word from the Holy Spirit, he told me, "God is about to start waking you up at night!" There was only one problem with that statement. If I never went to sleep, how could God wake me up? I sarcastically replied, "Great! That means He will actually have to put me to sleep!"

That same night when I laid my head onto the pillow, I fell asleep so fast that I couldn't finish this thought, "Am I really falling asleep? How is this hap...?" Then I fell fast asleep. Again, in a single, distinguishable moment, God destroyed a torment in my life and I've never had insomnia since. Not only did He redeem the years of exhaustion, but He also redeemed the years of loneliness and yearning for His presence. And He began to encounter me in the night!

REPLAY THE LOOP

God supernaturally freed me—*twice*! Being freed from the panic attacks and insomnia provided a lot of relief, and I should have used the interlude wisely—using all that breathing room to focus on defeating the other footholds. Instead, I became distracted by other areas of my life. This was a big mistake.

My friend Shamel Solomon is a Certified Personal Development Life Coach who focuses on inner healing and deliverance. Shamel once told me "Understand that distractions are only distractions if we allow them to be. When you disallow distractions, you go from being overwhelmed to overcoming because you can hear and see God clearly. I love the scripture in John 10:5–27. When distractions come up, I always say, 'I am God's sheep and I know His voice. I don't talk to strangers.' Simple yet effective to combating certain distractions."[4]

On the other hand, if we do not deal with the enemy's schemes, we leave room for distractions to take over our lives. Shamel goes on to explain the repercussions of allowing the enemy to overwhelm you with distractions. "If he can keep you overwhelmed and distracted, you can't think straight. You can't hear clearly. And you can't see right." One of the easiest tactics the enemy uses to overwhelm and sidetrack the believer is distraction. This is how the enemy kept me in a stupor despite being freed from so much. The next three years were so fast paced that I could only chew off so much at one time. Everything mounted and

---

[4] Solomon, Shamel, personal communication, paraphrased and used with permission. Learn more about Shamel at https://www. shamelsolomon.com.

moved at warp speed. I could only focus on a few things at once, and I chose the wrong things. The enemy took advantage of this.

Soon enough, I began to experience brand new torments that were the worst of all. Although it was a new torment, it felt like I was stuck replaying the same loop over and over again. This time, I experienced incidents of unexplained choking and strangulation. My throat would close up and choke itself over nothing. I would be in the middle of drinking water, and suddenly, I could not get my throat to swallow. I would be in the middle of a dinner or work meeting, and I would have food in my mouth, and it would get stuck. I could hardly breathe in these moments that sometimes lasted for minutes. I would be praying that someone wouldn't ask me a question because, for the literal life of me, I could not swallow. It was absolute insanity. My lungs had a similar problem, they would clam up under stress and anxiety. I felt a cage over my lungs and a noose over my throat. This was a terrifying combo. *I felt crazy.* This was a very strong attack on my life, on the call over my life to use my breath to preach the testimony of Jesus!

Instead of using the relief God had given me as an opportunity to choke the enemy out of my life, I just sat around and let the enemy do what he wanted. I was tired of fighting, I had no strength left, and I lacked a counter strategy. So, I became a sitting duck and a *pushover!* I passive aggressively allowed the enemy to take these footholds, and subsequently, he was able to set up strongholds. This went on during those latter years and the reason I never stood up for myself was because I was exhausted. *This* is the power of distraction and overwhelming a person. Most people in my life did not know about this struggle, and those who knew, they didn't know the extent of it because I rarely talked about it. When the episodes passed, my coping mechanism was to brush it under the rug, forget about it, and enjoy the moments when I had peace. This was a huge mistake—I was training myself to forget! Every day I didn't have a choking or breathing attack, I conditioned myself to *forget* they were operating in my life. In the times I didn't experience an attack, I delusionally thought I was free! Then, the next time the torment returned I was smacked upside the head as I relived the trauma as if it were the very first time. I also re-experienced the disappointment of feeling hopeless and powerless, so I hit "replay" on all the coping and forgetting behaviors like a terrible, reoccurring nightmare. I could not break the loop because I was distracted, overwhelmed, and unfocused.

AN IMPARTATION TO FINISH THE BATTLE

One day I received an impartation that changed everything. (An impartation is when something is given to you by another. In the Bible, we find that spiritual gifts can be imparted. In Romans 1:11 Paul says he wants to impart spiritual gifts to strengthen the believers, and in 2 Timothy 1:6 he reminds Timothy to stir up the gift that he received through an impartation from the elders.) I decided to attend a Christian retreat in Tennessee and during one of the services, Pastor Jennifer Eivaz invited people to come up for prayer. She felt prompted to release an impartation of what she calls "the writing sword"—an anointing from the Lord she herself is gifted with. Being a writer, I was one of the first people to jump up! Jennifer instructed those who had come up to stand in a line as she walked by and quickly laid hands on everyone with an impartation. When her feet turned to face mine, she paused. (I got butterflies on the inside and hoped to receive an awesome word from the Lord!) She laid her hand on my head, then she kindly and softly said, "It's like your mind has been hijacked. We take it back in the name of Jesus!"[5] After that, she imparted the writing sword anointing and moved on to the next person.

I thought Jennifer's word of knowledge was about anxiety, seeing as it was a turbulent time in my life. But to be sure, I just prayed for God to bring anything hidden into the light—because He always will.

HEARING VOICES: THE FINAL BATTLE

A short time after this, I started hearing outrageously offensive thoughts in my head. They were out of the blue and vicious. There is absolutely no fathomable way these unexplained thoughts could have been my own, so I just concluded I was supernaturally picking up on something in the atmosphere. I figured I was growing in the spiritual gift of discerning spirits, so I prayed a few prayers to settle the matter.

A week later though, it was much stronger—like hearing a voice inside my head instead of a thought. This was all in the middle of 2020 when literal chaos ensued from every possible direction. Not only were we dealing with a global pandemic, but the United States faced converging economic, social, political, and environmental crises! With all that was going on, I assumed I was picking up on the chaos and I took it as an assignment to pray for peace. I didn't think too much about it. Again, you can see, I did that thing where I smelled smoke and I dusted it under the rug because I was overwhelmed and unfocused. History repeated itself. That smoke turned into a wildfire that nearly wiped me out.

---

5   Eivaz, Jennifer, personal communication, paraphrased and used with permission. Learn more about Jennifer Eivaz at https://www.jennifereivaz.com.

THE ANTAGONIST REVEALED

One day I woke up to a message from my friend in Australia, Chantal Giannopoulos. In a positive manner, she told me she had a dream and would be praying for me. Chantal is a really wise intercessor. I've learned from her how to receive information from the Lord that may be concerning, but to deliver it with encouragement that quenches fear. She described her dream like this. The two of us were in the car with our mentor (Jennifer Eivaz, the pastor who had given me the word of knowledge and impartation of the writing sword). Suddenly, Chantal looked at me in the car and watched me shut down. *She said I could not speak, and I looked scared.*

Neither of us knew what this dream meant, but she knew to be praying for me in the days ahead. As for me, I felt so much comfort. I felt safe because I knew I was not alone, I had an intercessor and spiritual covering on the job. I felt confident in God's protection. He was clearly aware and not aloof to something going on, and He was surrounding me with prayerful help. Like the accident in Uganda, if He reveals a concern ahead of time, it's to give you peace in the midst of the situation and to assure you that you are safe and the Lord will help you. So while I wasn't worried, I knew to pay attention and increase my alertness.

About three days later I was scheduled to conduct a training in the community. This particular session would last three hours. I set up my equipment and then waited for the guests to arrive. I remember standing tall and at ease as the first attendees entered the room. *Then, out of nowhere, something I had last seen six years prior suddenly entered the room.* In disarray, I immediately recognized the familiar foe. I saw the blanket of darkness drape over the room the same as the first incident, but this time it was stronger, heavier, darker, and all the more brazen in its arrival. I was in shock as I stood trying to act normal in a professional setting while I suddenly found myself in the throes of a demonic assault. This was beyond my worst nightmares.

The heaviness it brought into the room had the effect of an atomic bomb. When it arrived, it nearly knocked me off my feet. It had a warping sound that announced its entrance and shivered me to my bones. Heaviness and fear hit me like a tidal wave. Suddenly, the voice I had been hearing for nine months started shouting in my head. It was at that moment when I realized the spirit that entered my life six years ago was the same spirit behind this new voice in my head. The culprit had revealed itself, and I was terrified. It took everything in me to not freak out in front of the guests that now spewed in one after another as I stood speechless in the doorway. It was so real, and it happened so quickly that I remember looking down at my feet and wondering, "What just happened? Did that really just happen? Did anyone else see it? Am I okay? Can they see it on me?"

The only thing that kept me calm was remembering Chantal's dream. I knew that if the Lord reveals it, He intends to deal with it. Still, I had a three-hour presentation to get through and panic was setting in. All I could hear was that nasty, demonic voice. I could barely think, see, or speak through the density of this evil spirit. I tried to go over it, around it, to get past it, but I was unable. It was like trying to talk over something screaming in my face, wincing to see past a thick cloud of smoke and struggling to hear through muffled waters. It was more than I could bear.

This subject is entirely teachable without my testimony, but there is a reason I'm sharing my story with such great detail. It is to expose the reality of how all the Devil needs is a single foothold to launch a spiritual siege over a person's life. If you would have told me a root of trauma and anger could give the Devil such a strong foothold that it would allow severe demonic torment for six years, I would not have believed you. In fact, I would have rebuked you for saying such a thing. Through my story and connecting all the dots and how they snowballed into a nightmare, my hope is to expose the fact that while footholds can create awful strongholds in your life, *they are defeatable*. Here's the catch: you can't defeat an enemy you won't face.

> ## *You can't defeat an enemy you won't face.*

When Jennifer Eivaz imparted the writing sword anointing to me, I wondered what got lost in translation. Because after my mentor prayed for me, the next thing I know is I'm hearing voices, seeing spirits, and getting pummeled into the ground. After that prayer in Tennessee, I was launched into the heat of a battle that I could never quite pin down because I couldn't figure out where the problem was rooted. Finally, the spiritual roots that had been covert for six years were forced into the open where I could hear them, see them, and defeat them—because they could no longer hide. At first, I thought something went wrong. Then I realized it was an ideal situation, as God was rounding up my enemies and forcing them out of hiding. It's easy to defeat your enemy in an open field when you're armed with a shotgun.

When I received the writing sword anointing, I should have realized that I had a writing assignment related to my battle. Looking back, I finally understood why the flood gate opened after the impartation of the writing sword. The writing sword is forged by finishing your battles. The impartation wasn't just to finish a book, but to finish a battle.

TRACE IT BACK

As soon as I completed the presentation (which was a bona fide flop), I rushed to the prayer center in town. I arrived feeling like a total failure, and I was desperate for God to help me. I needed answers for how that spirit had access to assault my mind like that. As a spirit-filled Christian, I wanted to know how it was able to torment me. I kept pressing God, asking Him in my state of utter disarray, "How did this thing get in?"

I had never met these prayer people in my life. I didn't tell the minister anything but my name. She didn't know a lick about what was happening. I just walked in, took a seat, and asked the woman to pray for me however the Holy Spirit led her. She spent a few moments praying in the spirit. Then, not knowing anything about me, she put her hands over my head and said to me, *"I see a cage over your mind, and I see trauma from Uganda."*

The meaning of Chantal's dream finally clicked. The Lord wanted to deal with the spirit of death and intimidation that attached to me from the car accident and tormented me with paralyzing fear in order to shut me down and shut me up.

Just like that, I suddenly knew everything I needed to know. In fact, I finally had proof for what I was afraid to admit: that first foothold had snowballed into numerous strongholds. Every single torment over the last six years—from the first panic attack to the choking, and now to this devilish voice in my head—they were all connected to the same spirit. Six years later, this prayer minister could trace the mental attack all the way back to Uganda—to the very first foothold of fear, bitterness and trauma. Back then, it would have been so much easier to deal with the flame when it was isolated and manageable. But I neglected to do so. Now, I had a raging wildfire on my hands. This is the danger of allowing the Devil to have one small foothold.

TACTICAL TRAINING

Drill In

For this training, we are going to change tactics and drill home three important points from this chapter.

Re-read: "What I would not let go of was the very foothold Satan grabbed onto."

Reflect: The believer is not meant to be easy prey for the enemy. The Lord's grace, mercy, love, and protection are far too great for us to be easy pickings. One way the Devil can grab a foothold on the believer is when we choose to cling to our sin and brokenness instead of giving it to God. Is there anything you need to give to God?

Re-read: "The enemy doesn't play fair, especially not on childhood brokenness, he takes the open doors where he can, and he's not above being untasteful about it."

Reflect: Jesus died to give you life in abundance, but the Devil will use and do whatever he can to steal, kill, and destroy that life from you. Take a moment to reflect and be honest about areas that you are not living the abundant life that Christ desires for you. How far back does this go?

Re-read: "You can't defeat an enemy you won't face."

Reflect: Christ has given you authority to cast out devils and overcome Satan. It's time to face what's been tormenting you and torment it instead.

Drill Out

No more being a pushover. Pray this prayer, or one in your own words.

I am a child of God and I have the spirit of adoption, by which I cry out to my Father (Romans 8:15)! I am an heir, and I will not be robbed of my inheritance. My inheritance in Christ is life in abundance, peace that is all surpassing, the authority to overcome the power of Satan, to continue Christ's work of miracles, healing, and deliverance, and to walk in power, love, and a sound mind (John 10:10, Philippians 4:7, Luke 10:19, John 14:12, Mark 16:17–18, 2 Timothy 1:7)! Lord, thank You that I have nothing to fear, for You are my protector and deliverer (Psalm 18:2). I decree and declare that the Lord is the only stronghold of my life, and all other strongholds must come down (Psalm 27:1, 2 Corinthians 10:3–5)! Lord, teach me how to pray as I move forward in tearing down demonic, fleshly, and ungodly strongholds (Romans 8:26, Luke 11:1). Open my eyes and ears and make me sensitive and discerning to what You want to do.

Drill Down

1 John 4:16–18   John 10:5–27

Luke 17   Romans 1:11

Psalm 16:7-8   2 Timothy 1:6–7

CHAPTER 4

Starting Line: Love and Power

When the Bible talks about a foothold, it means someone has you by the foot. There's another type of foothold, though, that I'd like for you to picture. Picture yourself climbing a rock wall. The goal is to climb higher until you reach the top. It's the same with our spiritual walk. We don't start climbing with Jesus just to go back down or to stay where we are, we climb with Him to go higher, on to better heights. The Bible puts it like this: we are being transformed "from one degree of glory to the next" (2 Corinthians 3:18 ESV). But in order to go from glory to glory, we have to make moves.

Imagine you are standing on the ground and looking for the rock you'll use for your first move. This is called "reading the route", the activity of approaching the wall and mapping out the climb. There are two ways a person can get on the wall, and that's either by grabbing onto a handhold or stepping onto a foothold. Which type of hold do you think is going to be closer to the bottom of the wall? Typically, a foothold is one of the first rocks a climber is searching for. Being closer to the base of the wall, a foothold literally gives you a "leg up" onto the wall. That initial foothold is *just a means to an end*.

Because that first foothold is really low on the wall, it's pretty easy to reach, so they have to make it a challenge for you somehow. What you will find is that those lower footholds are some of the tiniest ones you'll see. Some of those footholds might only be *centimeters* thick! They are so small that sometimes your foot slides right off! But here's the thing, it doesn't matter how small that starting foothold is because it's only a means to an end. It's an entry point. No one stays there longer than a second, they just use it as a quick access point to reach everything else! A skilled rock climber knows they only have to balance on that thing for a split second, and it's that split second that provides the launching pad for a hop to the next hold. All you need is a brief leg up so you can find a stronger hold.

Many times, we brush the small things under the rug, thinking they won't cause us harm. The enemy is hoping we gloss over or shrug off the small footholds. Over the years, the Lord has shown me how one small foothold is enough for the enemy. All he has to do is stand on that sad excuse of a pebble for a split second and by doing so, he latches onto the rest of that wall, and once he has the hold on us, he's not going to play fair for what he grabs onto next. (More on this later.) The teeny tiny footholds we excuse in our lives are the very entry points he uses to give him starting access.

What you are about to do is serious business. You are about to stand your ground and enforce the victory for your total freedom. But here's the problem: if you have footholds in your life that you haven't dealt with, the enemy is going to laugh at you when you show up to enforce your freedom. The enemy recognizes *authority*. If you haven't taken authority over your own flesh, sins, attitudes, and over your own self, how will you take authority over the enemy?

> **You know the enemy has a foothold on you when you find an excuse to make sin kosher.**

I realized I stood a better chance at defeating the enemy if I defeated my sin, my flesh, my soul, and the stubborn areas of my life that displeased God. I have heard of instances when someone was casting out a demon and the demon laughed in that person's face because they were still living a life of sin. The enemy will call the bluff in your authority if you haven't mastered your own flesh. You cannot walk in the fullness of your authority if pornography, sexual sin, lying, gossiping, and secret immoralities are casting shame over your life and driving you out of the secret place. I have learned you cannot please God if you do not love your family, honor your parents, or serve others according to their needs. You cannot please the Holy Spirit if you are offending Him because you think it's okay for the "woke" Christians—who are "free from religion"—to get drunk and high, or that you can be un-Christlike during business hours since you work in a cut throat secular environment. Even if you are pledged to be married, sex is not pure until that day. You know the enemy has a foothold on you when you find an excuse to make sin kosher. Then, when you are ready to be free, you will have to do the hard work of subduing your flesh before you subdue the enemy. If you try to confront the enemy and you have footholds of sin in your life, the enemy will laugh at you, because he has you subdued instead. We don't want that to happen. Let's get free and stay free.

The phrase, "On your marks!" is yelled to runners at the starting line of a race. It's a command to move them into their take-off positions. Before we start, there are a few pointers we need to cover so you don't lose your footing when you take off. If you've watched the Olympics, you've probably seen how a track star crouches down into a starting position. Before the invention of "starting blocks", some runners would dig a hole in the track, creating a foothold to dig their feet in. While this foothold gave them a footing, it held them back from a more successful race because it was a backwards hold instead of forward push. It wasn't until the early 1900's that the industry switched from a hole tucked into the ground to a launching pad. Now, runners use something called a "starting block". The starting block angles the runner's feet into flight, and when the race starts, you see them *leap* forward because of the "leg up".

HOW TO MAXIMIZE YOUR STARTING POSITION

You can run your race anyway you want to, but the person set on winning makes an effort to maximize their starting position. The starting block is said to give athletes a burst that propels them forward more quickly, putting them ahead of their competitor simply because of a stronger starting position.

I have three pointers, called the "don'ts", that will propel you forward in Christ's love and power. These three pointers will get you into a good starting position so that when you take off running, you'll leave the enemy in the dust. *On your marks!*

Don't Attempt without Christ's Love and Power

Philippians 3:10–11 says, "I want to know Christ—yes, to know the *power* of his resurrection and participation in his sufferings, becoming like him in his death, and so, somehow, attaining to the resurrection from the dead." This is how you know Christ; you must follow Him by taking up your own cross. We become like Christ in His death when we crucify our flesh. You cannot know Christ or walk in the *power* of His resurrection without dying to your flesh.

In Acts 19 some Jews tried to replicate Paul's authority over demons by applying the same tactics he used. They knew Paul cast out demons by using the name of Jesus, so they applied the same method, expecting to have the same result. If the name of Jesus was the only ingredient that mattered, the Jews would have succeeded in casting out that demon. They were surprised, then, when the demon laughed at them, pummeled them into the ground, and ran them out naked. If Jesus' name is all powerful, how come the misfire? The Jews said to the demon, "In the name of Jesus whom Paul preaches, I command you to come out."

Those Jews did not personally know Jesus. They tried to use an all-powerful name without the power that comes with personally knowing Christ (Philippians 3:10). The name of Jesus is all powerful, but if you don't know Jesus personally then you can't be a vessel for His power.

Christ's love in us is the conductor for God's power in us.

One component to walking in Christ's power is knowing Him. The other component is love. The two are one in the same. God *is* love, so when you know God, it is because you actually live in His love (1 John 4:16). These Jews, however, lacked power because they didn't know Christ's love like Paul did. If they knew Christ and knew His love *for* them and *in* them, they would not have used Paul's name as the conduit for Christ's power. In scientific terms, a "conductor" is a material (such as copper) that allows electricity to pass through it. There is actually a conductor for Christ's power. Ephesians 3:19 tells us *when Christ's love takes root in our hearts,* this is when we are *made complete* with all the fullness of life and *power* that comes from God! In other words, *Christ's love makes us complete in God's power.*

Christ's love in us is the conductor for God's power in us. If the name of Jesus was the only ingredient that mattered, these men would have succeeded when they spoke the name of Jesus. Instead, they used another conduit—Paul's name—attempting to reroute the authority through some other means because they lacked the necessary conduction for Christ's power. They did not know His love for them and in them, which means they lacked the source of Christ's power. If they knew Christ's love and power in them, they wouldn't have needed to use Paul as a conduit. They had good intentions, but the confrontation backfired so badly they left naked and battered. Demons know whether Christ's power is complete in you because it comes from His love taking root in your heart. You can't bluff authority because you can't fake intimacy.

If knowing God and living in His love is what gives us power, the other side of the coin is that we are *powerless* without knowing God and His love. One of the greatest threats in this regard is shame. Shame drives us away from God's love. Before Adam and Eve sinned, they walked with God, they talked with God, they were unclothed yet unashamed. But when Adam and Eve realized their sin, *they hid from God and covered themselves.* When we sin, our shame drives us to hide from God. It is in His presence that we receive His love. So how can His love take root in our lives if we are too ashamed to enter His presence? Without His love, His power cannot be made complete in our lives! *It's all intertwined.*

> *You can't bluff authority because you can't fake intimacy.*

James 4:7 says we should submit to God and resist the Devil. Submitting to God is your first step in subduing the enemy. When I was ready to take down this demonic attack in my life, I knew I was in a strong position to do so because I had already gone on a crusade against sin in my life, against the stubbornness in my flesh, and against the areas of my life that were so clearly not the fruit of the Holy Spirit. For those of you who have cleaned out your life and crucified the flesh, you have solid ground to stand on and shame has no hold over you.

But for those who are still struggling to beat patterns of sin, I encourage you to use the tactics in this book to go after your own flesh first. It is essential that you confront sin in your life, because if you do not, shame will drive you away from God, and it's knowing God and His love that makes His power complete in you (1 John 4:16, Ephesians 3:19). Brandon Gatson, founder of School of Reform, says, "God gives us no reason to run from Him, but every reason to run to Him."⁶ We are invited to approach His throne with boldness, it's His kindness that leads us to repentance, and it's His perfect sacrifice which makes us clean before Him (Hebrews 4:16, 10:10, Romans 2:4). Don't be run off by shame.

Lastly, I want to tell you something quite special to me, something that the Holy Spirit is allowing me to share with you. I witnessed something so personal to the heart of Jesus that I always have to pray before I share it—asking permission, checking my intentions, and listening for wisdom on how to share it. It's that precious and personal to Him. This vision happened by the leading of the Holy Spirit in my own personal prayer time, so you will want to measure it for yourself using the Word of God. The Bible speaks so much of the Holy Spirit being in us, but this vision confirmed to me what Jesus meant when He said to His disciples that we are also in Him, expressing, *"... you are in me, and I am in you."* (John 14:20).

One night in my prayer time, I saw myself laying on Jesus' chest, much like John the Beloved (John 13:23). As I laid my head on His chest, my ear became further pressed into His heart. And I heard Jesus' heartbeat. His heartbeat surprised me. I didn't hear a pulse; *I heard people.* It actually took my breath away, and it changed my life and the way I've come to love people. Listening to His heartbeat, I heard their first breaths, and their last. I heard their cries, their screams, their laughs, and their cheer. I heard their deepest grief and greatest joy. Not once did He take His eyes off of His people, His gaze was glued to

---

6   Gatson, Brandon. personal communication, paraphrased and used with permission. Learn more about Brandon Gatson at https://schoolofreform.com.

every moment of their lives. Without blinking, He watched the most exciting moments of your life, and even the drab days you so wish to skip through. It amazed me how Jesus was all-the-more devotedly present in the uttermost mundane and boring hours of your life. He is present in all.

Then His heart zeroed in on the cry that is in every man's heart. One we've all lifted up, asking, sometimes pleading, "GOD, ARE YOU THERE?". He lingered on this one, showing me person after person, each one uniquely searching for God from the depths of their soul—even those who did not know they were innately searching. His Word speaks of this in Isaiah 65:1, saying, "I revealed myself to those who did not ask for me; I was found by those who did not seek me. To a nation that did not call on my name, I said, 'Here am I, here am I.'" I looked up at Jesus, realizing His heartbeat was us, *His people*, and I said to Him, "You really love us, don't You?".

His name is Immanuel—God *with* us. How does one draw so near to God, as near as the one who was called John the Beloved, laying on the Messiah's chest? You become a beloved by *being loved*. God is love, and He *so loved* the world that He gave His one and only Son, that whoever believes in Him shall not perish but have eternal life (John 3:16). If you haven't given your life to Christ yet, I want to invite you to do so at this very moment. He's not just been waiting, He's been *longing*. His loving eyes have watched over you all your life. *You are in His heart.* I feel a prompting to tell you that if you feel tears welling up, tears are the expressionless words of the deepest part of your being, where your spirit is responding to what your soul can barely express. *God is real. He is love. He loves you. You are in Him, and He is in you.*

I also want you to know the important truth, the way to His heart. There is only one way to follow God, and it's not by saying a one-time prayer, it's by giving your life to Him over and over again, every day, for the rest of your life. This book will teach you how to cut off sin and live a fearlessly holy life, but you've got to count your previous life as a loss—or in Paul's words, "as garbage"—so that you may gain Christ and be found in Him (Philippians 3:8–10). Go now, and be found in Him from here on out.

He's already heard your cry, "God, are You there?".

He surely is, and He is crying out, "Here I am! I'm here! I'm here!".

His eyes have been on you every moment of your life. Can you give your every moment now to Him? I invite you to pause and give your life over to Him. It's simple, not complicated. Count your former life as a loss. Take up your cross. Follow Him each and every day, and be loved. You are a beloved. How wonderful. Eternal life is to know God, and you get to experience this today! I encourage you to call a Christian friend right now and tell them about the amazing decision you've just made, and watch God answer you, *"Yes, I am here! And you, my beloved, are my entire heart!"*

(Take your next steps at carastarns.com/knowgod)

Don't Be The Chicken

When the torments in my life snowballed into that final attack, I became *angry* at the Devil. I entered into prayer like a madman. I was clueless as to what weapon I needed, how to load it, and how to fire it, but that wasn't going to stop me anymore! I didn't approach the throne room with perfect footwork, good form, or a practiced target. I just came mad. I loaded that shotgun with every bullet I could find in the scriptures, and I started firing in faith. *I was even scared of myself!*

When I plotted out my strategy and began to execute it, the Lord told me how to win. In prayer, I heard, *"Wear him out!"*. He was explaining to me the tactic behind James 4:7 which says, "Resist the Devil, and he will flee from you." Demons don't flee from you if you ask nicely, and they often don't go on the first command. They must heed authority at some point, but they are first and foremost rebellious spirits, so they test your authority and see if they can push back. Some spirits are so strong Jesus said they only come out with fasting and prayer. Sometimes when we say, "I command you to leave!" and the spirit doesn't leave, we think we don't have the authority or power. This leads us to quit way too many battles prematurely because the enemy didn't obey on the first command, or within the first five minutes! We have to quit treating these spirits like they heed to a code of honor. *They are disobedient and rebellious spirits.* They *will* resist you.

When I say they recognize authority but also disobey, I am not contradicting myself. When you quit prematurely and don't stand your ground, the misfire is because *you* don't recognize *your* authority. When a rebellious child disobeys his mother, does she back down? Absolutely not. She digs in her heels all the more! She looks that child in the eyes and says, "Excuse me, I am your mother, and you *will* do what I say. And if you don't obey right now, the consequences will be even worse for you." She will say this as many times as necessary until the child submits to her authority.

Authority is asserted when you don't take "no" for an answer, and you stand your ground until that thing submits. So, when you back down prematurely, *you* aren't asserting *your* authority. And if you aren't asserting your authority, you shouldn't expect a disobedient spirit to comply so easily. We should not expect a demon to behave by any other nature. A rebellious and disobedient spirit is going to be just that! They are stubborn and difficult, and they test authority.

When you open the scriptures, the demons that Jesus confronted back-talked Him, resisted, pitched a fit, prolonged their exit, and tried to stay in their "house"! Let me show you in scripture. In Mark 1 a demon interrupted Jesus' sermon by causing a disruption in the synagogue. The spirit yells in the middle of the service and begins to brazenly confront Christ. Then, when the demon is cast out, the spirit doesn't just leave on a dime. First, the spirit screams, then throws the man to the ground and convulses him before leaving his body. This was a disruptive spirit who pitched a fit before obeying. In Mark 5 a demon actually back-talked Jesus! Jesus told the spirit to go and the spirit didn't budge. Instead, he dragged out his exit for as long as he could. When Jesus tells him to leave the man, the spirit begins to shout in the middle of a crowd, yelling, "What do you want with me?". After pitching a fit, which doesn't work for him, he resorts to begging. The spirit pleads, "In God's name don't torture me!". In Mark 9 the spirit wouldn't leave before harming the boy so badly that after the episode, the child appeared dead. This is the nature of a demon; they rarely go peacefully and without resistance. So if Jesus experienced back-talking and rebellious spirits, we have to anticipate that we will too. (More on this later.) This is what the Lord was preparing me for when I heard, *"Wear him out!"*. You have to wear out the Devil. You wear him out by resisting him.

But resistance is not passive. Have you met those Christians who say, "Stop glorifying the Devil by talking about demons!"? These people think that if we address demonic presence and activity, we are glorifying Satan or giving him too much credit. This is quite wrong. The teachers of the law (aka the die-hard religious folk) accused Jesus of casting out devils by the power of Satan. In other words, deliverance came across as demonic to them! (Are we stuck in the same thought pattern today?) But Christ responded by telling them that deliverance is actually the very sign that proves God's kingdom is among us! Jesus said, "But if it is by the Spirit of God that I drive out demons, then the kingdom of God has come upon you." (Matthew 12:28).

Many Christians think that if you pay too much attention to the demonic, this draws attention to Satan and glorifies him. Consequently, such a person thinks it's better to ignore the demonic. I agree there are many who need to be re-guided in regard to over-attributing many of life's problems to the demonic. But there is actually the same amount of ignorance and danger in totally ignoring the demonic. *Resisting the Devil does not mean avoiding eye contact.* It does not mean ignoring the enemy who comes to steal, kill, and destroy when God has given you authority to bind, trample, and overcome (Matthew 18:18, Luke 10:19)!

Resisting the Devil is not passive. Resistance, by definition, involves violent opposition! You don't turn the other cheek to the Devil. You don't ignore the thief, hoping he goes away soon and doesn't steal anything valuable—while you hide in the closet praying that he doesn't kill you! Resistance is not waiting it out and avoiding confrontation. Resistance is aggressive. Resistance applies pressure and *holds* that tension until it pushes back the opposition!

The Lord showed me a vision of the game that kids play in the summer pools, the one called "Chicken Fight". In this game, teams of two stand facing each other. One person stands in the water while their partner balances on their shoulders and wrestles the opposing team. You win the game by knocking the other team down. The Lord showed me that if I could just wake up every morning and apply pressure without letting up, that the enemy would topple over, and I would win. You see, the Devil is betting you'll tap out first, and he's usually right. We often tap out when we experience any kind of resistance—we immediately doubt our power when the rebellious spirits rebel! We tap out so quickly when we don't see those instant results, and we weasel out when we're tired.

Yet the golden strategy is so simple: *Resist!* Hold that tension! This is a cause-and-effect scenario. If you submit to God (step one is critical) and resist the Devil, then he *will* flee. Friend, you don't need perfect form. You don't need fancy moves. All you need is Jesus, a no-quit attitude, and persistence.

Another game, simply called, "Chicken", is a dangerous game between two cars. While I hope that no one actually plays this game, I've seen it in the movies. In this case, two cars speed toward one another and the first person to swerve is the "chicken". This is what God showed me behind the meaning of James 4:7. The enemy is the chicken. *He will cave first* because we have the power of Christ in us and all we need to do is hold our position. *Victory is already ours; we just have to enforce it!* But so often, we let the enemy win a match that he is destined to lose—all because we don't know how to stand our ground for as long as it takes. Sometimes it takes a while! You are both resisting one another. You are resisting the Devil's schemes, and the Devil is resisting your authority.

Ryan LeStrange is the founder of the Global Hub in Atlanta and has authored numerous books pertaining to spiritual warfare. In one of his sermons Ryan says, "You must resist long enough and strong enough".[7] Someone has to buckle first. How strong willed in the spirit are you?

---

[7] LeStrange, Ryan, paraphrased from a Global Hub sermon and used with permission. Learn more about Ryan LeStrange at https://www.atlhubchurch.com.

The flesh is weak, *but* the spirit is willing (Matthew 26:41)! You need a strong-willed spirit to outlast a stubborn devil. I didn't have much to show in regard to my fighting record, I just knew the loser caved first. So, every morning, I told the Devil, *"It won't be me."*

James 4:7 tells us the battle move. Resist the Devil! What do we do when the enemy doesn't respond the first time that we command him? *We resist!* What do we do the second time we command him, and he blows his tongue in our face? *We resist!* Do we reconfigure the approach if he doesn't listen on the next command, or the tenth day, or the third week? No, the tactic is the same. Stand your ground, hold the line, and resist him! If you are submitted to God and you resist the Devil, he *will* flee. Don't let up on that resistance until the enemy falls back. *Wear him out!*

Don't Bootcamp Trauma, and Don't Enlist a Broken Heart

Before we proceed any further, it is very important that I speak to the need to slow down and walk through any inner healing that needs to take place. This book very much fasts forward to the freedom chapter of my story, but there was a much longer healing chapter. During those earlier years, I could not fight even if I wanted to. I was physically beat down by a back injury and PTSD from the accident. I was spiritually beat down by the anger I carried against God and the confusion I had at that time about the direction of my life. Emotionally, I was at an extreme low. I was so depressed I spent most of that first year sleeping off the thought of preferring to be dead. I could barely make it out of my room those days. I had no fight in me, *and the Lord had no intentions to drive me into battle in this state.* What a truly good Father He is!

> ## *He makes us rest. (Psalm 23:2)*

Me, on the other hand, I was the one trying to run right back into battle. I remember balling my eyes out on the floor of my bedroom as I told the Lord, "I just want to be fixed!". (It was definitely a recurring appeal.) It was me who was not comfortable being broken before the Lord, but the Lord was pleased to comfort His daughter. *He stopped me from sending my trauma to bootcamp.* I wanted to ship off my brokenness, make it do a few pushups and laps around the field, then send it back home in better shape. I thought God wanted a soldier. I was so wrong. He longed to comfort His hurting daughter. Many tears were cried during those years, and there were so many layers, processes, steps, and seasons to my healing. When we are worn out, He is the Father who takes us on excursions to be restored beside green pastures and quiet waters. In fact, Psalm 23:2 says He *makes* us rest. This is how the soul is restored, through rest. "He makes me lie down in green pastures; He leads me beside quiet waters. He restores my soul…" (Psalm 23:2–3).

God used those years to teach me about the jarring repercussions of trauma. I expected God to speak to me about needing spiritual healing, but I was surprised by how much He spoke to me about needing healing in my mind, body, and soul. At just the right time, I came across a book called, *The Body Keeps the Score*, by Bessel van der Kolk[8]. When I was dealing with panic attacks I could not explain, Bessel revealed to

---

8 van der Kolk, Bessel. *The Body Keeps the Score: Brain, Mind, and Body in the Healing of Trauma* (2015), https://www.besselvanderkolk.com/resources/the-body-keeps-the-score.

me that trauma can change the chemistry and structure of a person's brain. Psychologically speaking, trauma can alter absolutely anything. Taking your "normal" and crushing it, mauling it to shreds, flipping it upside down, and spinning the lottery wheel for what you're taking home with you. For one person, this wheel of "misfortune" might land on mental blackouts and dissociative behaviors; for another, it could be crippling panic attacks and depression. We don't get to choose how trauma impacts us. Trauma assaults a person's brain by remodeling neuropathways, chemical compositions, and age-old structures at a moment's notice. When this happens, we don't get to order "normal" off the menu anymore. What comes to the table typically catches a person off guard.

Imagine the route you take every morning for work. Based on how many times you've taken this path, you know what you'll see, how many lights and intersections you'll come across, and exactly where and when to dodge potholes. It's a predictable path that you've learned to navigate safely. But say there's been terrible damage to the road—overnight it was eaten up by a sinkhole or demolished by a giant milling machine. You can't cross that road like normal because there's been a trauma to the path, so you're unexpectedly forced off the road. Off-roading is unpredictable, it's a path you take when your normal one is destroyed, and you're forced to find another way to move forward.

Our brain has "roads" as well, called neural pathways. Trauma has the power to alter these neural pathways, which can lead to an off-road experience we refer to as PTSD. This figurative off-roading is just as bumpy, scary, dicey, and unpredictable as the real thing. You never know what you'll encounter down the road, and there's no consent forms or liability waivers. Trauma takes you off-road without your permission.

PTSD can also be compared to the aftershock of an earthquake. While the first earthquake (being the initial trauma) has long come and gone, there may be aftershocks that come in waves for days, weeks, and even years to come. There is no way to know how many aftershocks will hit or when they'll occur (i.e., panic attacks, dissociation, depression, resurfacing memories, etc.). While my rational mind understood that I had emerged alive out of the accident, my body was telling me a different story: I was stuck in trauma!

Many times, we walk off injuries without realizing our body needs time to recover in ways we cannot see. We go on with our lives and expect our body to do so as well. Consider a bruise, it's an internal healing process that takes place after an external injury. When we bump into a table corner, we move on after the initial surge of pain wears off. We shake off the injury, forgetting all about it. But when a bruise appears, we may find ourselves wondering how it got there. Then recollection sets in, and we say to ourselves, "I totally forgot I was hurt." We may even be surprised how something that seemed so little at the time, even caused the bruise. While we want to move on from the injury like nothing ever happened, our body is left in the aftermath and needs time to heal. This is Bessel's main point: the body keeps the score. Even if you've long forgotten the incident, your body remembers.

I didn't know I had PTSD until a month after the accident. My "bruising" showed up four weeks later. (The deeper the injury is, the longer it may take for the bruise to appear at the surface.) I am thankful that my church was the driving force behind the recovery steps that I took. It required time, finances, professionals, grace, patience, and tears. I leaned on a Christian counselor, my mentors, and my pastors to process my experiences and emotions. I found a psychiatrist and a doctor to help me restore my brain and body to order. In those early years I needed to heal spiritually, emotionally, and physically. It is important to use a multi-disciplinary approach to diagnose, treat, and heal your wounds.

One of the best books I've read on trauma's intertwined relationship with the spirit, soul, and body is by Jennifer Eivaz, titled, *Inner Healing and Deliverance Handbook*. By sharing her own story of occultic childhood trauma, she discusses the importance of having a healing plan that involves biblical and practical tools for bringing your heart back to life.[9]

Healing is part of the ministry and comfort that the Father provides to us. But because of this mistaken view I had of God wanting a soldier at all times, I ran myself into the ground in the beginning of things. I thought I was more useful to God as a trooper, so I wanted to stay strong. This distorted my identity for years. In His beautiful grace, the Lord slowed me down so I could really press into this area of healing in my heart. He never once dealt with me like I was needed for battle. He never once dealt with me like I was an injured or unfit soldier who needed to be discharged from serving in His army. Instead, He met me on the floor of my bedroom, and He laid my head on His chest and He *told* me to cry. I didn't want to cry, so He actually pleaded with me *to* cry. I cried for years. I cried the tears I never cried in my childhood. I cried the tears of feeling abandoned and rejected by God because of the trauma I experienced. I cried the tears from trying to be a good soldier all my life, not realizing I ran that broken little girl's heart into

---

9   Eivaz, Jennifer. *Inner Healing and Deliverance Handbook: Hope to Bring Your Heart Back to Life* (2022), https://jennifereivaz.myshopify.com/collections/books/products/inner-healing-and-deliverance-handbook-hope-to-bring-your-heart-back-to-life

the ground. I didn't come to know the power of Christ in me during an epic battle, I encountered His power in me by realizing my identity as a daughter, and this came through the lowest point of my life, marked by tears of brokenness that I cried in His arms. Before the Lord led me into the battle for freedom, He first tended to my woundedness so I could be *healed*.

Be sensitive to letting *Him* do the heavy lifting. The strategies in this book are powerful and effective, they will help you fight with biblical weapons and with Christ's love, power, and authority! But if you sense you are in a season where you are meant to cry on His chest, then please don't run a broken heart into the ground by trying to run into battle. If you try to fight on an injury, you might make it worse—or you might just get yourself killed. Don't be so focused on winning battles that you forget who you are to God. It's not the heart of the soldier He is drawn to, *it's the heart of His child.* Don't enlist a broken heart into battle when He's trying to minister that heart back to life through His love and comfort. Healing and deliverance work together—but this does not equate to speed. Healing takes time and you will find yourself working through different layers, seasons, and needing to rest at every stage. We want to shout at strongholds, but with certain ones, you may need to start with tears. Don't bulldoze a wrecking ball into a stronghold of trauma until the Father has delivered you out of that tower. Your heart and emotions need comforting, don't forsake them to the rubble of demolition.

TACTICAL TRAINING

Drill In

Read: Philippians 3:10–11, Acts 19:13–16, Ephesians 3:15–19

Reflect: When Christ's love takes root in our hearts, this is when we are made complete with all the fullness of life and power that comes from God! In other words, Christ's love makes us complete in God's power. This is your inheritance as a child of God, to be filled with His love and power. When it comes to casting out devils, the reason you can't bluff authority is because you can't fake intimacy.

Read: James 4:7, Mark 9:14–29

Reflect: Jesus demonstrated how to deal with stubborn and rebellious demons who wouldn't go on the first command. He didn't panic, give up, or question His authority. He stood His ground. He taught the disciples how to troubleshoot when a demon is disobedient, affirming to them that certain demons are stubborn and take extra measures to come out (prayer and fasting).

Is there possibly a demon or demonic plot in your life that won't budge? What would an aggressive, militant resistance against the Devil look like for you?

Read: Psalm 23:1–6

Reflect: When life has been hard on us, we tend to develop thick skin to become our armor and defense. We turn into our own protectors, fighting and fending for ourselves. By doing this, we not only remove God from His role as protector in our life, but we also overexert ourselves and run our traumatized and weary hearts into the ground. Our Father is the God who makes us lie down in green pastures. Is there anything God wants you to rest and heal from? Take a moment and ask Him.

Drill Out

The Devil wants to see you fall on your face as soon as you take off running. But now you know the essentials to a strong starting line. Is there anything else that would hinder you from finishing the race? Has the torment, weariness, or storms of life made you doubt God's love for you? Has sin and shame driven you away from His presence?

Remember, if knowing God and living in His love is what gives us power, the other side of the coin is that we are powerless without knowing God and His love. Don't let anything hold you back from His presence. Be still and ask the Holy Spirit to highlight anything on His heart for you. And close the book to spend some time in His presence.

Drill Down

2 Corinthians 3:17–18

Hebrews 4:16

Hebrews 10:10

Romans 2:4

Galatians 5:22–23

John 14:20

Isaiah 65:1

Mark 1

Mark 5

Matthew 12:28

Matthew 18:18

Luke 10:19

Matthew 26:4

Psalm 23:2

CHAPTER 5

Deliverance is a Miracle

If you are reading this book, there is a good chance you have some type of stronghold in your life that you have yet to overcome. You've taken all the steps you can think of and yet anxiety, stress, over-thinking, anger, pain, bitterness, backtracking, self-harm, self-hatred, addiction, sin, and disease remain—none of it will lift from you, nor from your family line. I understand what it's like to speak the name of Jesus over something, to receive prayer for breakthrough, to apply faith, to renounce-repent-break curses, and to see nothing happen. (Later in the book, we will cover how to destroy stubborn strongholds and why they require persistent pressure. Don't be discouraged by past attempts.) I understand what it feels like to give up after so much hard work and disappointed hope. Disappointment can cause us to give up prematurely.

When people don't see strongholds budge, there comes a point when they rationalize that it's just their own personal "thorn in the flesh" and they accept it as a carnal weakness. Or they might write it off as an "effect of the fall of mankind", experiencing unfortunate factors and tragedies out of their control. Believing this, they accept that the stronghold will just be a part of their life. I understand because I camped there for many years. Many of us have concluded that our woes are uncontrollable and unbeatable, they're just part of carnality and a fallen world. But what if this thing in your life is actually a stronghold? That would be good news to the oppressed person, because we have weapons to bring it down! How would you know it's a stronghold? The only way to find out is to take a battering ram to it and see if it begins to splinter.

In this chapter, we are going to ask a lot of questions along the lines of "what if" and "could there be". What if there was a spiritual stronghold behind the issue? Could there be a spiritual root to the problem? If the therapeutic and medical arenas have not been able to put a dent in this thing, what do you have to lose by trying one last measure? What do you have to lose by trying out the tactics in this book, to apply your weapons of warfare to a potential spiritual stronghold, and seeing if something begins to crack? If your weapons of warfare can tear it down for good, your entire life could change. You could be free!

CARDS ON THE TABLE

We are all dealt a hand of cards. These cards are dealt to us through life's dealings, made up of family, culture, surroundings, networks, biases, and most influential of all, through experiences. Some of these cards that have been dealt to us should not be in our deck and should be discarded, these are the Jokers. In some games, Jokers can be played as wildcards and placeholders to the real thing. But we don't want wildcards and placeholders in our hand. I invite you to put your cards on the table and to examine what's been slipped into your hand by life's dealings. Are there Jokers that need to be discarded?

The Joker cards represent the lies of the enemy. There are believers who omit anything they want from the gospel and submit their own wildcards and placeholders in lieu of the truth. There is an entire movement in the faith that is doing this openly and receiving applause for it. What's been reproduced is a false gospel that has been remixed to serve the self, to be palatable to people who won't yield their hang-ups, and to be more inclusive and accepting. (We are not accepting people; we are accepting sin.) When we remix the pure gospel because it doesn't work for us, we let in compromise, deception, and heresy. We have to be careful what beliefs we let slip into our hand.

Pastor Tim Jones, author of *Extreme Sheep*, said to me, "I am actually finding that most people are so hungry to represent God to the world, that they've represented God to the world based on the world's terms."[10] This is the nature of the progressive movement, since the world has rejected God, they present God to the world based on the world's terms so people will be more inclined to receive Him. They promote a "come as you are" invitation to catch the masses but never present the call to repent and come into the fullness of who God created us to be. Therefore, we are catching masses, and not only do they come as they are, but they stay as they are, which is not the Gospel of Jesus Christ because the fruit of His Gospel is a transformed life. But it's not just the progressive movement that is omitting entire branches of the gospel, this is happening across many believers, churches, and

---

10 Jones, Tim, personal communication, paraphrased and used with permission. Learn more about Tim at https://www.campusthirst.org/about#PASTORTIMJONES.

denominations, even the ones who protect the integrity of God's word so tenderly.

What comes to mind is a modern day "spiritual hippie" movement. We have a bunch of spiritual hippies who love peace and hate war. You've heard them before, they say things like, "I don't want to glorify Satan by talking too much about what he's doing, let's talk about what God is doing", "I want to focus on the positive and not the negative," "Let's talk about God's power, not Satan's power," "If I leave Satan alone, he will leave me alone", and more mumbo jumbo along those lines. These are spiritual hippies, they are great at parties but are terrible friends to have when you're in a battle like I was—where I saw, heard, and was physically assaulted by evil spirits!

The first lie we must consider discarding is the lie that the spiritual realm is not real, and neither is spiritual warfare, and neither is Satan. A study published by The Barna Group in 2009 found that only 26% of American Christians strongly believe that Satan is a living being. The rest strongly disagree, or truly have no idea where they stand, which tells us the majority of the church is amiss to the reality of spiritual warfare and our charge to be armed and on guard. Consider these results:

> *Four out of ten Christians (40%) strongly agreed that Satan 'is not a living being but is a symbol of evil.' An additional two out of ten Christians (19%) said they "agree somewhat" with that perspective. A minority of Christians indicated that they believe Satan is real by disagreeing with the statement: one-quarter (26%) disagreed strongly*

and about one-tenth (9%) disagreed somewhat. The remaining 8% were not sure what they believe about the existence of Satan.[11]

This is where American Christianity stands, utterly divided and confused not only about spiritual warfare, but whether or not Satan exists, although the Word of God is crystal clear on the matter. Have you ever wondered what scams Satan has been running amok? Just survey believers! This poll reveals to us exactly where he has focused his efforts across the Western Christian church—which is in convincing us that he isn't real and we needn't be bothered by the thought of him.

Before germs were discovered, doctors argued amongst themselves about why people were getting sick, how disease spread, and how to fight an enemy of whom they had no knowledge of. Those who claimed there must be an invisible and common enemy were pegged lunatics in the scientific and medical fields. Come to find out, an invisible and common enemy truly was to blame. Germs were finally discovered in the late 1600's. Whether or not a person believed in germs did not spare them from infection. In fact, their oblivion caused more harm because physicians would practice without proper sanitation and risk themselves further. If you think not believing in spiritual warfare keeps you safe, you are mistaken. Spiritual warfare does not spare you because you don't consider Satan to be real or on the prowl—as the Bible assures you, he is.

---

11   Barna Group. Used with permission. *Most American Christians Do Not Believe that Satan or the Holy Spirit Exist* (April 13, 2009), https://www.barna.com/research/most-american-christians-do-not-believe-that-satan-or-the-holy-spirit-exist/.

The spiritual hippie believes that once you come to Christ, there's no spiritual warfare because Christ defeated Satan at the cross. Christ's "finished work" doesn't mean we no longer have problems with Satan, rather, His finished work allows us to take every weapon that is formed against us and to cast it down by enforcing what Christ did for us. Revelation 12:11 says we overcome Satan by the blood of the lamb and the word of our testimony. *One is a finished work, and one is still in the works.* Jesus' sacrifice is finished, but your testimony is a continuation in which you get to apply the name of Jesus, the blood of Jesus, your faith, weapons, and armor to hurl down the enemy on a daily basis.

Pastor Tim Jones grew up in a conservative background that steered far away from the topic of spiritual warfare. He told me, "Intellectually, I was repulsed by the idea of spiritual warfare." It was halfway through his lifetime when things shifted. As a pastor, he came across countless people who were hurting, broken, and tormented. These people desperately needed freedom, but out of everything that was being done for these people, at the end of the day, nothing worked. As a spiritual father, He saw people in bondage and the heart of a father for his spiritual sons and daughters cried out to God, pleading, "There has to be more!". Looking into the life of Jesus is what shifted Pastor Tim. After so many years of being repulsed by the thought of spiritual warfare, what drove him into the biblical worldview of deliverance was his *compassion*. It was actually the very same story with other mothers and fathers in the Bible. These parents had children in tormenting bondage, and despite their unbelief and skepticism regarding spiritual matters, their compassion for their children is what drove them to Jesus for deliverance.

In Matthew 15 Jesus ministers to a group of Jews when a Canaanite woman brazenly comes into close proximity to Jesus and His inner circle. Having a Canaanite woman in their midst was a big faux pas, considering the Canaanites were deemed enemies to God. Being in their midst was daring enough, but then she crosses the line even further. As a Canaanite and a woman, she breaks every social queue and societal rule by crying out to Jesus! The disciples leap into action as bodyguards and crowd-control, and they whisper in Jesus' ear, "Lord, send her away! She keeps crying out to us". In other words, their prejudice meant to say, "Lord, this vile woman won't buzz off. Shouldn't we see her out?"

But this was no ordinary woman who could be silenced or overlooked. This was a mother, and mothers bear another kind of audacity when it comes to advocating for the needs of their children. The mother continues to disrupt the meeting, causing an uncomfortable distraction and drawing attention to her unwanted presence. By shouting loud enough for everyone to hear, making herself all the more detestable to the surrounding Jews, she begins to plead her case. "Lord, my daughter is demon possessed and suffers terribly, help her!" After some back and forth, Jesus remarked to her and to the crowd about her great faith, then He delivered her daughter right then and there.

Consider this thought. Do you think it was easy for this mother to accept the fact that her daughter suffered from a demon? Absolutely not. How uneasy this mother must have felt to realize her precious daughter had a demon problem. But which of these two thoughts is more terrifying? The fact that a person is tormented today, or that they will be tormented endlessly for the rest of their life if we do not help them? We have to become more concerned with people's freedom than our comfort. What if this mother didn't want to admit her daughter was demonized, what if that was too much for her to acknowledge? What would have happened if she misdiagnosed the spiritual problem for a natural matter? Perhaps writing it off as such for peace of mind, as spiritual hippies tend to do. The only way this mother would have peace of mind was by seeing her daughter set free, even if that meant coming to terms with the fact that a demonic matter was at hand. I want you to underline this point: it was the mother's compassion that propelled her forward, to see her daughter delivered.

In Mark 9 the attention shifts to a father in the same position. The scene begins with a large, fussy crowd. When Jesus is seen coming their way, the crowd hushes their argument, but Jesus insists, "What is it that you were arguing about?" The father immediately begins to describe the situation. I want you to take note of this: while our culture wastes time arguing about whether or not a person can be tormented by a demon, their culture argued like this, "Why won't this demon leave? Well, who can cast it out? What can we do? Where is the Rabbi they call Jesus?" Their argument was not about whether or not a child or believer could be tormented, rather, the heated debate was centered around a solution for freedom. While we argue about the existence of the problem, they argued about how to resolve the problem. "That command didn't work; what can we do now?" How much more I would rather be in that type of argument—processing deliverance as a group who is learning through trial and error—because at least everyone is in one accord for the sake of freedom!

This father was struggling with unbelief. He was found arguing among the crowd about the flopped methods that had led to his unbelief and hopelessness. When Christ walked up, the father could have packed up, gone home, and spared himself from the disappointment of yet another failed attempt to deliver his son. This father was in front of the man he hoped could deliver his son, and yet because of past attempts, he carried belief and doubt all in the same moment. He came up with the most truthful and desperate words a double-mind could ever speak, pleading, "I believe! Help me overcome my unbelief!". He did not let the disappointment of past attempts, or his growing unbelief hold him back. His compassion drove him to surrender to a radical thought—maybe my son can be free after all!

Notice how compassion drives us toward deliverance, even if the process has hiccups. If you feel repulsed by the thought of deliverance, I invite you to consider the matter of people's freedom with the heart of a mother or father. There are people who desperately need freedom. They have tried every method under the sun but after years of hard work they are not free. People are living in torment, in bondage, cycles, and patterns that are destroying lives and derailing destinies. I invite you to look upon these people as your own children. Don't you want them to be free? When a Canaanite mother was despised in a crowd and turned away, she did not let rejection and prejudice stop her. No matter how embarrassed or offended she felt, her compassion for her daughter's life drove her to demand freedom. A mother or father does not care about what deliverance looks like, about how many times it takes, how many past attempts failed, or how many hiccups occurred in the process. They just need it to happen so their child can be free! What if we all looked on deliverance with the heart of a mother or father? How many more children would be free?

This is the heart of a person who wants to see people set free: full of compassion and driven to the biblical worldview of deliverance. A Pharisee will see deliverance and accuse God's work of demonic influence. But a father will see an opportunity for deliverance and cry out, "Help my unbelief, so my child can be free!". I implore you, for the freedom of your sons and daughters, and their sons and daughters, that you would look on the work of deliverance with the heart of the father in Mark 9. Knowing his mind can hardly come to terms with the spiritual matter at hand, he turns his unbelief over to Christ in exchange for breakthrough and freedom for his child! There are generations counting on you to stand for this branch of Christ's ministry.

PHYSICAL HEALING THROUGH SPIRITUAL DELIVERANCE

Here's another question I want you to consider. While a person may have a real condition (be it physical or psychological) could there be a spirit behind it? Could there be a demon problem behind the problems of the mind and body? The Bible is clear on this matter, and the answer is yes, there could be. In fact, some of Jesus' deliverances are double-documented as healings. The father who brought his boy explained to Jesus that his son had been mute since childhood. Not only was the boy mute, but he had problems on the psychological level as well. The demon would bring on terrible seizures and even force the boy into self-harm and suicide attempts, throwing him into water and fire to be killed. This is the kind of patient we send to high level psychiatric wards for intense around the clock treatment, sometimes for a lifetime! People are living a life in bondage, and one simple question could be the key to a treatment that actually works, "Could there be a spiritual problem behind this?"

To ask whether there is possibly a demon problem to a health problem is not to dismiss, ignore, or minimize a very real health problem as only a spiritual issue. I want to show you that in many cases, Jesus and the disciples weren't dealing with "one or the other". It does not have to be "either/or" because sometimes it is "both/and". If a health problem has a spiritual root, that does not mean the health problem is not real and does not need professional treatment. It certainly is real and does need professional treatment. To diagnose a health problem as a potential combination with a spiritual matter is simply to diagnose the need for a multi-disciplinary approach, meaning you will combat the matter through both physical and spiritual treatment. I had severe PTSD, anxiety, panic attacks, insomnia, and I was hearing voices and seeing spirits, which is typically diagnosed as psychosis. These are all real mental health conditions for which I sought professional treatment. But these conditions had a spiritual root, and when I introduced a spiritual treatment to what I was already doing, this is when I was freed *and* healed.

Freedom and healing go hand in hand. Acts 10:38 says Jesus *healed* those who were *oppressed* by the Devil. Why doesn't this verse say Jesus freed the oppressed and healed the sick? If Jesus was healing, shouldn't the verse state that it was the sick who were healed? Yet it says the oppressed were healed.

Oppression takes on many forms, including mental and physical illness. Pay close attention to how the Bible documents the deliverance accounts. In regard to the mute boy, Luke 9:42 says, "Jesus rebuked the impure spirit, healed the boy, and gave him back to his father." In this case, the muteness and the psychological insanity were explicitly tied to the demon. Jesus first cast out the demon then He healed the boy. The Canaanite girl was freed and healed in the same exact pattern. The girl's mother said she was demon possessed, but when Jesus freed her, He deemed her healed. Matthew 15:28 says, "And her daughter was healed at that moment." What we have here are two cases when a demon problem was double-documented as a healing. The Greek word being used in these two accounts is "iaomai", which means to heal—generally of the physical, sometimes spiritual—disease. Matthew 15:28

and Luke 9:42 expressly state that a demonized person was healed of their suffering and disease. *When they were freed of their demon problem, they were healed of their physical and mental problems.* Sometimes the two are intertwined.

> **Freedom and healing go hand in hand. Acts 10:38 says Jesus healed those who were oppressed by the Devil.**

Jennifer Eivaz has such a testimony. In an article titled, *Can Physical Ailments Have Spiritual Roots?*, she shares her story of being healed from scoliosis. Her back problems started in elementary school, so she began seeing doctors to monitor the issue. The curvature worsened in her mid-twenties so badly that she struggled to walk. She could barely lift her legs at the end of a long day and was forced to shuffle her feet just to get anywhere. As the problem progressed, she lost so much strength in her back that sometimes she would fall over while sitting. Some of Jennifer's greatest passions include exercise, running, and surfing. To experience such a devastating condition in her mid-twenties must have been horrifying. She found doctors and therapies to stop the damage and manage the condition, but she also began to pray. It was while reading in the book of Psalms one night that her eyes were opened, she writes. She made the connection between her back problems and the difficult upbringing of her childhood, and she saw the Lord was ready to cut the cord of wickedness off of her back (Psalm 129:1–4). She asked the Lord to "cut the cord" and she felt something actually snap off of her back! After that, her spine began to contort back into place.

She has been free of pain ever since.[12] You can read this story and more like it on Jennifer's website (www.jennifereivaz.com).

Jennifer puts it this way, "Almost every physical issue that I've ever had to battle had a spiritual root and was more than just a physical problem. At the same time, each issue had a medical diagnosis. A name, a description, and a suggestion for medical treatment. I discovered, however, that physical issues with spiritual roots do not respond well to medical treatment, or they come back, until the root has been dealt with."

In Acts 19:12 the Bible speaks of unusual miracles, including the mass-miracle that occurred by passing around handkerchiefs that had merely touched Paul. The believers took these handkerchiefs to the sick, this was a prayer tool they used to reach countless sick people when they were too weak to travel to the ministry meetings. Notice the notion here was to heal the sick. Acts 19:12 says, "the diseases left them and the evil spirits went out." Again, we see another direct correlation between deliverance and healing working in tandem. We do not know how many of those people had only a disease and no evil spirit. It's possible that some may have received only physical healing, but based on the purpose of the handkerchief, which was taken specifically to heal the sick, this account is expressly remarking that evil spirits left the sick people. Matthew 8:16 says that many demonized people were brought to Jesus, and this is what He did for them, "...he drove out the spirits with a word and healed all the sick." Again, we see another example of healing working with deliverance, and deliverance working

---

12   Eivaz, Jennifer, *Can Physical Ailments Have Spiritual Roots?* (December 18, 2019), https://www.jennifereivaz.com/post/can-physical-ailments-have-spiritual-roots.

with healing. When there is a spiritual problem behind a physical one, we must be freed to be healed. Deliverance is a miracle, and sometimes, it doubles as a healing miracle.

When demons come to torment a person, they don't just come to scare you in the nighttime, they come to ruin your life. We see in these cases a person (children, to be exact!) had a physical and/or psychological problem that was directly tied to a demon. When they were freed, they were also healed. I invite you to consider these questions one last time. What if a condition actually has a spiritual problem behind it? Could there be a spiritual root to sickness, disease, patterns and cycles, or strongholds in your life? Lastly, what do you have to lose if you try applying a spiritual treatment alongside the professional treatments you are already using? Remember the heart of the father, who cried out, "I believe; help me overcome my unbelief!" Sometimes we just need to ask Jesus for a little help to try things one more time, and one more way.

THE BELIEVER IS THE TARGET

If we are filled with the Holy Spirit, how do demons get access to the believer? Through the soul. In Acts 4 we see a community of believers who are selling their possessions and property to meet the needs of those who are in lack. This community is an example of what happens when everyone in the group becomes filled with the Holy Spirit. There was so much harmony with one another that all the needs in the community had been wiped out!

After describing this community that was incredibly filled with the Holy Spirit, the writer goes on to talk about one of the church members who became filled with Satan. Peter is baffled, wondering how someone who is filled with the Holy Spirit could also be filled with Satan. He asks the question like so, "Ananias, how is it that Satan has so filled your heart that you have lied to the Holy Spirit…?" The word that Peter uses to ask how Satan has filled Ananias' heart is the same Greek word he just used in the previous chapter to say the entire community (including Ananias) had been filled with the Holy Spirit. Peter had the same question many of us have today, "How can you be filled with both the Holy Spirit, and with Satan?". Ananias was a believer, a committed member of the church, and he was filled with the Holy Spirit. (To say he was not a true believer is to say that any Christian who sins and falls to selfish motives is not a true believer. We all fall short.) When he saw the other believers pitching in their property and possessions, he wanted to contribute. But instead of being entirely truthful about the matter, he told a lie. So was he full of the Holy Spirit, or full of Satan? Was he contributing to God's work, or was he serving himself? Again, it is not a case of "either/or" but "both/and". Ananias was trying to be part of the body of Christ in his giving, but the enemy grabbed onto soulish footholds of greed, selfishness, and deceit. This is one example of a Holy Spirit filled Christian who was filled not only with the Holy Spirit, but also with Satan. Both can occur. Even though the Holy Spirit occupies our spirit, the enemy can still come into our lives through sinful areas of the flesh and soul.

In 1 Thessalonians 5:23 Paul writes about us having a spirit, soul and body, and tells us that God sanctifies us "through and through". The Holy Spirit is able to sanctify every part of us, but our soul is the determining factor as to how thorough this sanctification goes. Consider what Paul writes in Romans 8:5, "Those who live according to the flesh have their minds set on what the flesh desires; but those who live in accordance with the Spirit have their minds set on what the Spirit desires." Notice that the middle man is the *soul*. Your soul is your mind, will, and emotions. These are the things that make you uniquely you, and they are powerful determinants in your life. According to Paul, the soul (mind) determines if you live according to your spirit or according to your flesh. In the next verse, he says one course leads to life and the other to death. In Romans 8:7 he adds that the mind set on the flesh is hostile to God and is incapable of submitting to God. There was a believer in the Corinthian church who would not turn from his sin, so Paul remarked that even though the man's sin had handed him over to Satan for the destruction of his flesh, the church hoped (perhaps through the man's faith, or future repentance) that his spirit would be saved in the day of the Lord Jesus (1 Corinthians 5:5). The enemy looks for areas of the soul to grab onto, because even though we might make it to Heaven, it will be as one barely escaping the flames (1 Corinthians 3:15), and we will have missed out on a life fulfilled for God.

It is totally possible to be saved, born again, with your name written in Heaven, and to still have demonic footholds and strongholds creep into your life. I was saved and filled with the Holy Spirit while seeing and hearing evil spirits! I never questioned whether or not I was filled with the Holy Spirit. My life was clean, and doors were shut, so I looked for the trapdoor those evil spirits crawled through. I was surprised to learn that my soul (mind, will, and emotions) had opened a door through rebellion and stubbornness from the orphan spirit. The Bible says rebellion is as the sin of witchcraft, and stubbornness is as iniquity and idolatry (1 Samuel 15:23 [NKJV]). When I found the breach, I sealed it shut and exterminated any who squeezed through. Having a demonic presence lurking in my life never made me question my salvation. In fact, I took it as a sign that the enemy must have wanted to sift me because of the calling over my life to serve God!

The mix-up for many people is they don't believe Christians can be possessed, which is true. To be clear, a demon cannot have possession of your spirit. Possession implies ownership, and a demon cannot own you because the blood of Christ paid for you to belong to Him. In this vein, no, a believer cannot be possessed by a demon. While "demon possession" is documented in the Bible in plain English, the word choice is a poor translation. The Greek word "daimonizesthai" is where we've gotten our word for "demon possession".

According to Derek Prince[13], a better translation would be afflicted by a demon or subjected to demonic influence. I think most of us can agree that a Christian can be afflicted or influenced by the enemy. This is why a Holy Spirit filled Christian can be snagged by an advertisement for pornography; they are filled with the Holy Spirit, but that advertisement they saw for pornography grabbed onto areas of the soul and caused the person to go back into old cycles. Although we are sealed with the Holy Spirit (Ephesians 1:13, 4:30) we can still be subjected to the influence of other spirits, such as the spirit of lust.

Isaiah Saldivar (renowned preacher and host of the Revival Lifestyle Podcast) poses the question this way, "The proper question is this; not that a Christian can be demon possessed, but rather, can a Christian have a demon or be under the power of demons? The answer is yes."[14] This is why Satan entered Judas when he made up his mind to betray Jesus. This is why Christ looked back at Peter and called him "Satan"

---

13   Prince, Derek, summarized from sermon, *How To Be Delivered From Demons* (November 5, 2019), https://youtu.be/nqAGdE6l_Js.
14   Saldivar, Isaiah, paraphrased from *Revival Lifestyle Podcast* messages and used with permission. You can listen to them at https://revivallifestyle.libsyn.com/. You can learn more about Isaiah Saldivar at https://www.isaiahsaldivar.com.

when he tried to prevent Christ from the cross. Years later, this is why Peter looked at a generous but lying Ananias and asked him, "Why has Satan filled your heart?" Lastly, this is why Paul predicted that Holy Spirit filled believers were going to fall away from the faith, because of deceiving spirits influencing them (1 Timothy 4:1).

For some Christians, they believe the Devil will leave them alone as long as they leave him alone. Do you know that by just being a born-again Christian you are interfering with demonic strongholds and assignments? Just by being you! When Christ was in the synagogue one day, He was merely preaching. He wasn't operating in signs or miracles yet, and He wasn't even casting out devils. He was preaching a sermon and minding His own business when a demonized man stood up and demanded, "Why are you interfering with us?!" The enemy doesn't leave us alone if we "mind our business". The reason the enemy came to sift Peter is because of the very call on his life to build the church. The enemy sifts us in order to derail Kingdom destinies.

> *We are in a spiritual battle, against spiritual foes, and spiritual schemes— and the believer is the target.*

If the Devil cannot interfere with a Christian, why did Satan himself interfere with Christ, the son of God, for 40 days? The Devil worked hard during those 40 days. When he failed to thwart Christ, Luke 4:13 says, "When the devil had finished all this tempting, he left him until an opportune time." The Devil is looking for opportunities to interfere in your life, actually, he's waiting for the right opportunity to thwart your destiny. 1 Peter 5:8–9 tells us the Devil is looking for someone to devour, and this is a problem among believers. Unbelievers were not mentioned, because it's the believer who is the threat, not the unbeliever. The mention here is to alert believers to a waiting and watchful enemy, who is looking to pounce and devour you. This sounds a lot like Luke 4:13, the enemy is looking for an opportune time.

Ephesians 6:11 says the Devil schemes against us. This is exactly why we've been given armor and weapons—to stand our ground against him, and to stand firm. But here's the problem: if you don't think you are in a battle, you let down your guard. Can you imagine what God thinks about this? Through the use of countless scriptures, He has prepared us to defend ourselves, and instead, we've let down our defenses. God wants you to know that we are in a spiritual battle, against spiritual foes, and spiritual schemes—and the believer is the target.

DO NOT DISCOUNT TESTIMONY

Even though a scriptural study proves that the Devil is targeting believers, there is shockingly still so much debate in the church about whether or not a believer can be tormented. Because the deliverance accounts that are documented in the Bible are so brief, there is much more to learn about how demons come into our lives and begin to take footholds and build strongholds. The objection for many people is that we shouldn't expand into a broad and thorough teaching on spiritual warfare based on biblical accounts that are particularly brief. I understand the notion, but it's entirely unbiblical in nature. Expanding our understanding, our works, our signs and miracles, and the use of our authority is the privilege of being a new-covenant Christian! That being said, there are certain basics of salvation that should never be expanded on. Ephesians 4:4–6 says, "There is one body and one Spirit, just as you were called to one hope when you were called; one Lord, one faith, one baptism; one God and Father of all, who is over all and through all and in all." These are the essentials of God's salvation for us that we should never change, edit, add to, delete, alter, or expand upon. But there are other matters that we are going to have to work with the Holy Spirit on, because where the Bible ends is where we begin.

> *Sometimes we will come into a fluke, a hiccup, a flop, and the answer is to always go back to Jesus for continued training and instruction. In order to do the Lord's work, we have to work with the Lord.*

Just before Jesus ascended into Heaven, He told the disciples that certain signs will follow the believer, and the very first sign to follow the believer was driving out demons! In Mark 16:17 Jesus mentions it first, "And these signs will accompany those who believe; in my name they will drive out demons..." Remember, the disciples didn't have a perfect streak of success. Why do you think their errors and hiccups are documented in the Bible? To teach us how to work through them, and the answer is going back to the Master.

One time, the disciples could not cast out a stubborn demon. Despite all of the training they had received from the Master, their best attempt was still a flop against this strong spirit. They returned to Jesus and asked why they could not cast it out, seeing as they had cast out so many other demons before. So what did they do? They went to the Lord to work through it. Jesus told them, "This kind only comes out with fasting and prayer." Sometimes we will come into a fluke, a hiccup, a flop, and the answer is to always go back to Jesus for continued training and instruction. In order to do the Lord's work, we have to work with the Lord.

Mark 16:20 tells us how the disciples proceeded in the works of the Lord, telling us, "Then the disciples went out and preached everywhere, and the Lord worked with them and confirmed his word by the signs that accompanied it." The Lord works in signs, wonders, miracles, tongues, and deliverance all for the purpose of confirming His Word, and He does this by working with us. Anyone who casts out devils is working with the Lord. As we work with the Lord, He guides us, instructs us, and helps us to "work through" dead ends and flops when we come into a new challenge.

Why do we have more teachings on deliverance today than what is written in the Bible? Because we are fulfilling a work that was purposed when Jesus ascended into Heaven and sent the Holy Spirit. As 21st century believers, collectively, we have 2,000 years of working with the Lord under our belt! Yes, we can build on our understanding of deliverance beyond the brief accounts in the Bible because we've been working with the Holy Spirit to fulfill His command for the new covenant believer, which is that we will do even greater things than Jesus did (John 14:12)! We can conclude that by doing greater things, we will have more experiences, and those experiences come with a wealth of knowledge and insight—more than what is briefly documented by the New Testament church, which only encapsulates the lifetime of the disciples! What kind of powerful church would not have more understanding of deliverance and miracles after 2,000 years of working with the Lord? (What an absolute shame that would be, let us not allow our generation to be that shame!)

We have to remember that our testimony plays a valid role in drawing conclusions about our faith and how God operates in the ministry of signs, wonders, and miracles (Remember, deliverance is included! Mark 16:17). In the Revival Lifestyle Podcast, Isaiah Saldivar explains the validating effect of a person's testimony[15]. Isaiah points out that when John the Baptist had a dying wish—to confirm whether or not Christ was the Messiah—Christ did not send an answer but a testimony. While John was in prison, he sent his disciples to ask Jesus if He was "the one" they had been waiting for. Jesus did not answer yes or no, instead, He told the disciples to relay their own message through the conclusion of what they had seen and heard. In other words, John should base his conclusion on the individual testimonies of the disciples! Jesus replied, "Go back and report to John what you hear and see: the blind receive sight, the lame walk, those who have leprosy are cleansed, the deaf hear, the dead are raised, and the good news is proclaimed to the poor. Blessed is anyone who does not stumble on account of me." (Matthew 11:4). Here, we see Jesus sanctioning us to draw conclusions based on the testimony of believers!

---

15 Saldivar, Isaiah, paraphrased from *Revival Lifestyle Podcast* messages and used with permission. You can listen to them at https://revivallifestyle.libsyn.com/. You can learn more about Isaiah Saldivar at https://www.isaiahsaldivar.com.

> *An expanded understanding of miracles should credit the believer, not discredit them.*

The Bible does not spend long on the deliverance accounts, but after 2,000 years of "God working with us", and proving Himself through deliverance ministry, we've come to know a thing or two. *This is sanctioned.* An expanded understanding of miracles should credit the believer, not discredit them. The believer's testimony is an acceptable component to teaching on deliverance ministry when it's in line with scripture and harmonizes with the testimonies of the collective group! The disciples taught on their experiences. In fact, they went to great lengths to share and compare notes on their experiences. They held special sessions and meetings, traveling far and spending long amounts of time together to compare their own personal experiences so that the collective group could combine their experiences to gain a greater understanding about how God moves and works. We overcome the enemy by the blood of the Lamb and the word of our testimony (Revelation 12:11). A testimony is born from your own personal experience and turns you into a deliverer! You've been empowered to hurl down the enemy through your testimony, and to tell others what you have seen and heard. I guarantee you; someone needs to hear your testimony so they can believe for theirs!

DELIVERANCE IS BAKED INTO THE CHILDREN'S BREAD

Some Christians just don't like deliverance, and others don't think it's for the saved believer. For the former, I find the matter to be related to underlying grievances about how deliverance ministry occurs—mainly that it can be messy, crazy, intense, difficult, and it can appear out of control. We know this to be true according to the nature of demonic manifestations that Jesus dealt with—those spirits caused distractions, threw fits of rage, pouted with intense begging and emotional outbursts, backtalked with ploys of stubbornness, threw people to the ground, tossed them around, seized them and caused loud shrieks and foaming at the mouth. All that being said, yes, sometimes deliverance can appear out of control, but this is the *illusion* the demon wants to cast so that bystanders will feel unsettled and shut down deliverance ministry. Let me show you such a case in the Bible.

One such deliverance resulted in a grumbling mob after Jesus freed a man from a legion of demons. This man had been lurking among the tombs and was possessed by demons so violent that no one could pass through the cemetery. When Jesus freed the man, all of the demons fled into a herd of pigs that then ran off a steep bank and drowned in a lake. This must have been a terrifying sight. What really scared them, though, according to Mark 5:15 is this, "When they came to Jesus, they saw the man who had been possessed by the legion of demons, sitting there, dressed and in his right mind; and they were afraid." Not only were the people afraid of how the deliverance happened, but they were afraid of a changed man coming into their midst, one who previously terrified them. Afraid, the disgruntled townspeople drove Jesus away!

This story is not only an incredible documentation about deliverance, but also a biblical example of a group of people who chased out the deliverer because the deliverance upset the comfort of their personal lives and the makeup of their social circle. They would rather have their pigs and their lives back to normal than for this man to be free and walking among them. There are believers who want to protect the orderly branches of Christ's ministry, the ones that are easily presented and explained, the ones that are well received, but they omit the branches that are more on the "rough" side because people have complaints about how it goes a little sideways sometimes—like down a river bank! Deliverance can be messy, but it is not out of our control. This may have been the point that Jesus wanted to make, something He wanted to expose about the heart of man. Remember, the demons did not go into the pigs without first getting Jesus' express permission. They asked Jesus if they could enter the pigs and Jesus agreed. What we come to find out next is that the people would rather have demons and pigs in town than a deliverer! How many other people could have been delivered had they not kicked Jesus out of town?

If you are a believer, deliverance is part of your job! Mark 16:17 includes it in our job description. I invite you into the biblical worldview that deliverance is for the believer, in fact, it's the children's bread. This is the note I want to end on.

In the story of the Canaanite woman who cried out for her daughter to be freed, Jesus speaks of the *children's bread.* In calling Jesus the "Son of David" the woman was recognizing Him as the Messiah who was promised through the line of David. When she calls out, asking for His mercy, Jesus replies, "I was sent only to the lost sheep of Israel." In saying this, He is expressing that He was sent specifically to the Jews. Nevertheless, she persists, begging, "Lord, please help me!". Finally,

Jesus introduces the subject of the children's bread. What I want you to realize in the back and forth between Jesus and this woman is what the children's bread represents. After the mother called out to Jesus for deliverance and acknowledged Him as the Son of David, Jesus replies *by referring to Himself,* saying, *"I was sent…".* The banter continues. The woman addresses Jesus again, asking for Him to deliver her daughter, and this is when Jesus answers her by switching from talking about Himself to talking about something called the children's bread.

Although He switches to a metaphor, Jesus is still referring to her plea for deliverance, and still referring to Himself. This lines up with John 6:35 when Jesus said, "I am the bread of life. He who comes to Me shall never hunger…", and again with the breaking of bread, saying, "This is my body, which is given for you…" (Luke 22:19). When Jesus speaks of the children's bread to the Canaanite woman, we see Jesus using yet another picture of being our bread, which provides for the needs of our lives. In this case, the need is for deliverance. *Jesus* is the children's bread, one who was *sent to help,* and who is able to give the bread and feed those who ask.

So just how does this bread feed the children? Following Jesus' line of thought, He told the woman He was sent, and we know exactly why. Jesus tells us in Luke 4:18–19, announcing, "The Spirit of the Lord is on me, because he has anointed me to proclaim good news to the poor. He has *sent* me to proclaim freedom for the prisoners and recovery of sight for the blind, to set the oppressed free, to proclaim the year of the Lord's favor." This is why Jesus was sent. These are the works He was anointed to accomplish and the central mission was *freedom*! Have you come across a church that won't allow deliverance because, "It's not safe for the children to see" or it's "Not appropriate for children"? Remember, Jesus casted devils out of children. Jesus is the children's bread, sent to free the oppressed, giving the children's bread to God's children. What He gives you is *good*. Mark 7:9–11 says, "Which of you, if your son asks for bread, will give him a stone? Or if he asks for a fish, will give him a snake? If you, then, though you are evil, know how to give good gifts to your children, how much more will your Father in heaven give good gifts to those who ask him!"

If Jesus gave you bread to eat, would you reject His gift? Of course, you wouldn't; you would take and eat. Have you ever met a picky eater who doesn't like certain foods and won't let them touch? They use their fork to separate the foods they dislike into a reject pile on their plate. The way bread is made, though, all the ingredients are mixed together. You cannot separate the flour from the salt, either you will eat it or you won't, because you cannot pick it apart. Jesus told us why He was sent, and you cannot separate His mission to bring the good news from His mission to bring healing and deliverance (Luke 4:18–19). If you truly want to partake in the children's bread, you have to take and eat it the way Jesus serves it. The Gospel doesn't take special orders for picky eaters, it's already crafted to perfection for your nourishment. Deliverance is baked into the children's bread, and it was made with *compassion*. Deliverance is central to Christ's mission, and an equal part of the miracle branch, along with healing, signs, and wonders! Jesus says that whoever is casting out devils is performing a miracle. *Deliverance is a miracle; and it can be your miracle.*

TACTICAL TRAINING

Drill In

Read: Luke 4:18–19, Mark 16:17–18

Reflect: After reading these scriptures, would you agree that deliverance was part of Jesus' mission on earth and ministry to us? Consider that Jesus healed and delivered because of His compassion for people.

Right now, you may be reading this book because it is you who is in need of healing and deliverance, but can you see how you are also called and authorized to do the same for others?

Read: Luke 11:14–23, Matthew 8:28–34, Matthew 12:32

Reflect: Jesus had to explain to critics that casting out demons was a sign of God's kingdom. After Jesus delivered a disturbed and violent man, the people begged Him to leave town. They would rather have a demon possessed man running amok in town than have their pigs running off a cliff. By their attitude, the people ran the deliverer out of town.

How many more could have been delivered? The Lord desires to set the captives free. We have to consider that our criticism of deliverance is criticism of the Holy Spirit, and when we run off the deliverer, we forsake the oppressed to their bondage.

Read: Matthew 15:21–28, Mark 9:14–29

Reflect: As you read over these deliverance stories, what stands out to you? A mother broke through social and cultural faux-pas' to see her daughter healed and delivered. A father was found passionately arguing about his son's deliverance, while also feeling doubtful and hopeless. These parents were dealing with strong obstacles of culture and doubt. They stormed these barriers and broke past them because of their compassion for their children.

Consider this thought: what if the church became so compassionate about those who are in bondage, oppression, and demonization that we became fiercely adamant about seeing every person delivered?

Drill Out

Are you more like the mother, who is ready to push her way to the front and break all social rules to see a deliverance? Or are you more like the father, who has some unbelief and previous disappointments to overcome? Spend some time in prayer and ask the Holy Spirit to prepare your heart for a deliverance miracle in your life.

Pray this prayer, or one in your own words.

> *Lord, You said that anything is possible for the one who believes (Mark 9:23). I believe You are my deliverer. I don't want to live in bondage. I don't want to live in oppression, heaviness, weariness, torment, or affliction. I want to serve You and live for You without hindrance. I believe Your sacrifice on the cross set me free. I also believe You gave me authority over all the power of the evil one. Open my heart to my authority as a believer and teach me how to use biblical weapons and tactics to overcome the enemy.*

Drill Down

Acts 10:38	1 Corinthians 3:15
Luke 9:42	1 Samuel 15:23
Luke 4:13	Ephesians 1:13
Luke 22:19–20	Ephesians 4:4–6
Psalm 129:1–4	1 Timothy 4:1
Matthew 8:16	John 14:12–14
Acts 4:12	Matthew 11:4
1 Thessalonians 5:23	Mark 5:15
Romans 8:1–8	John 6:35
1 Corinthians 5:5	Mark 7:9–11

CHAPTER 6

Surprising Obstacles

In the book of Acts, we find the apostles going about their ministry of healing, casting out demons, and preaching the Gospel of Jesus Christ. The religious leaders warned them to stop, and when they did not, the apostles were thrown into jail (Acts 5:18). However, in the middle of the night, an angel of the Lord broke them out! The angel opened the doors of the jail, brought them out, but before releasing them, the angel told them to go and preach the "message of life" (Acts 5:20).

When God breaks us out of prison, He doesn't free us so we can go into hiding and keep a low profile for the rest of our lives. God breaks us out of prison so we can preach the "message of life"! This message of life will break others out of prison too! I knew I was bound in a deep, dark dungeon. I knew I didn't belong, but I had no idea how to break free. Fortunately for us, we have a God who when we cry out to Him, our cry reaches His ears. He sends forth His love and faithfulness for us, and He rebukes those who hotly pursue us (Psalm 18:6 and 57:3). That's our God!

When I read that the apostles were broken out of jail so they could preach the message of life, I realized I did not have that message. I believed it was real, but it was not in my belly, and this message certainly didn't have dominion over my life. If I had the message of life burning in me, I wouldn't be choking, I wouldn't be spinning out, I wouldn't be drowning in a vortex of panic attacks and fear. If I had the message of life, even an ounce of it, I knew I could break the Devil's hold in my life.

As I began dreaming about my freedom, I started to dig deep and look for the roots of all these issues. I wanted to know how these things had such "strong holds" over me. I wanted to know how they got their power and how I could destroy them. I found what I was looking for when I read 2 Corinthians 10:4–5, which says we have weapons of warfare that are not carnal but mighty in God. *According to scripture, these mighty weapons have the ability to tear down "strongholds" and every high thing that exalts itself against the knowledge of God.*

Bingo!

Suddenly, it dawned on me. I realized every stronghold in my life had actually become an obstacle, and this giant obstacle had set itself up against my knowledge of God. It's a catch-22 situation. These strongholds blocked me from my knowledge of God. And without the knowledge of God, I did not have the weapons, faith, or understanding I needed to destroy those pesky strongholds! I was stuck. This is why the enemy will use a stronghold and wedge that towering thing between you and your knowledge of God. The enemy is attempting to *barricade* us from the knowledge of God, because without it, we are powerless and empty handed. In Hosea 4:6 God attributes the destruction of His people to their lack of knowledge. The right kind of knowledge has the power to give you militant advantage, while the lack thereof will lead an entire people group to extinction.

Our knowledge of God arms us for victory. When you truly know God, you cannot help but to know your *identity* and *power*. When you know who you are in God the promise of freedom will register so deep that you no longer put up with footholds, strongholds, or assaults of any kind. The Bible says that you are free and you must not return to slavery or oppression. When you know who you are and the power God has given to you, you don't dare hand over your authority or freedom. I lacked all these things, which told me I lacked the knowledge of who God is and what He has done for me!

When this realization hit me, I got out a pen and paper and I traced the strongholds in my life all the way back to a lack of knowing God. This exercise may benefit you just the same (you'll find it at the end of this chapter). In dealing with the panic attacks and choking, this was related to *fear*. In allowing those demonic spirits to (visibly!) wash over my life like a dark curtain and speak things to me, I did not have a sound mind, instead, I had a mind that was driving me into *mental insanity*. In being a pushover to these spirits, I demonstrated spiritual *timidity* and *powerlessness*.

It was plain as day. These demonic torments had been set up as strongholds to block me from having the knowledge of God, because the knowledge of God totally *opposes* fear, mental insanity, timidity, and powerlessness. 2 Timothy 1:7 says, "For God has not given us a spirit of fear, but of power and of love and of a sound mind." (NKJV). I was living the opposite of what scripture told me I was designed to live! This happened because the enemy wedged strongholds and obstacles to block me from my knowledge of God. I experienced a "Woah!"

moment when I realized every stronghold in my life could be destroyed by simply knowing who God is and standing firmly on His Word.

I began to flip through the pages of scripture and search for the weapons of warfare that are described in 2 Corinthians, the ones that could actually tear down strongholds. This was not a valiant process, but a desperate one. Guess what: it makes no difference to God! In fact, the Bible tells us His power is made perfect in our weakness. Although I had been a Christian my whole life, I had used the Bible as a crutch instead of as a weapon, so I wasn't sure what I was looking for when I went to find my weapons of warfare. I started in Ephesians where Paul tells us that we are not in a carnal battle, but a spiritual one. When I realized that Ephesians 6:17 says *we have a sword of the Spirit for spiritual battles,* I did a double-take! I had been a Christian my whole life so I can't tell you how many times I had read Ephesians 6:17. The difference at this time in my life was I knew I was experiencing a spiritual battle. It was undeniable. I understood this verse in a whole new light and I thought to myself, "I have a spiritual sword for spiritual battles? That's great news. I have something to use!"

I immediately went into prayer to deal with the enemy, but I quickly learned something about the sword of the Spirit. I expected this weapon to afflict the Devil, but I didn't realize how much this weapon would actually afflict me, and my own soul. Hebrews 4:12 supports this claim, expounding, "The word of God is living, and powerful, and sharper than any double-edged sword, piercing even to the division of soul and spirit…" God's Word is a mighty weapon that has the ability to sever between your soul and spirit. *Ouch.* You need to be prepared for the severing, so let's unpack this some more.

Let's make a clear distinction between soul, spirit, and body. 1 Thessalonians 5:23 distinguishes and also links all three, saying, "May God himself, the God of peace, sanctify you through and through. May your whole spirit, soul and body be kept blameless at the coming of our Lord Jesus Christ." This verse indicates that a person is made up of three parts—spirit, soul, and body. Each one is distinct from the other. When Paul says we must be sanctified "through and through", he is drawing attention to the three components that make up the human and that God works His way through each layer.

So where does each layer begin and end? Your soul is the essence of your humanity and how you express yourself. It is composed of your mind, will, and emotions. You think, feel, and make decisions through your soul. Your spirit, on the other hand, is how you connect intimately with God. Proverbs 20:27 explains that when God connects to the deepest part of you, He does this through your spirit. The verse reads, "The human spirit is the lamp of the Lord that sheds light on one's inmost being." In the same way we are connected to our natural parents through birth, we become connected to our spiritual Father by spiritual birth. In John 3:5–7, Jesus says, "'Very truly I tell you, no one can enter the kingdom of God unless they are born of water and the Spirit. Flesh gives birth to flesh, but the Spirit gives birth to spirit. You should not be surprised at my saying, 'You must be born again.'" Jesus said the Holy Spirit lives in us, and Paul said the Spirit becomes sealed with us (John 14:17, Ephesians 1:13).

If the Holy Spirit seals Himself to us, no wonder He wants to sever between soul and spirit! He wants us to walk entirely by the Spirit. Galatians 5:25 says, "Since we live by the Spirit, let us keep in step with the Spirit." So then everything we do is by the leading of the Holy Spirit. It is by the Spirit that we worship, understand, and connect with God. John 4:24 (NKJV) says, "God is spirit, and his worshipers must worship in the Spirit and in truth." 1 Corinthians 2:11–12 also says, "For who among men knows the thoughts of man except his own spirit within him? So too, no one knows the thoughts of God except the Spirit of God. We have not received the spirit of the world, but the Spirit who is from God, so that we may understand what God has freely given us."

Lastly, the body is what we live in right now. We know that our bodies are made of dust and will return to dust, and in Heaven we will receive new heavenly bodies (Ecclesiastes 12:7, 2 Corinthians 5:3). To summarize, you are a spirit who has a soul and lives in a body. (You are also born again and sealed up with the Holy Spirit in order to connect to your Father.) The question then becomes; If God designed all three of these components to make up the human being, why would He want to crucify the flesh and sever between soul and spirit? *Because He must sanctify each one distinctly.*

For God to sever between our soul and spirit means He must have a good reason to do so. Remember, your soul is made up of your mind, will, and emotions. Would you agree this trio is strong, persuasive, and convincing? Absolutely, and the mind is the strongest rudder in the group. Reading Romans 8:5–8, I want to show you that your mind is the middleman of your flesh and spirit. It acts as the referee, determining who gets the ball. Take a look.

> *Those who live according to the flesh have their minds set on what the flesh desires; but those who live in accordance with the Spirit have their minds set on what the Spirit desires. The mind governed by the flesh is death, but the mind governed by the Spirit is life and peace. The mind*

> *governed by the flesh is hostile to God; it does not submit to God's law, nor can it do so. Those who are in the realm of the flesh cannot please God. (Romans 8:5–8)*

As you can see, your mind determines if you live by the spirit or by the flesh. Your mind is the middleman who referees between "team death and hostility" and "team life and peace". It is the rudder that decides if you go the way of the flesh or the way of the spirit, and this is why the sword has to sever between soul and spirit—because your mind (soul) will try to dominate!

When I began tearing down those strongholds, I quickly realized how much my own flesh and soul had contributed to the Devil's masterpiece. This is hard to admit, but it's true. When the Word of God told me I did not have a spirit of fear, I stood facing that stronghold with Ephesians 6:17 and Hebrews 4:12 as a sword wielded in my hand. I was poised to swing my sword and destroy those strongholds, but I was surprised by the obstacle that stood in my way. *It was my own soul and flesh, standing in the way, begging me, "Please, don't hurt us!"*

Since your flesh and soul lead to death, they must be crucified and severed, respectively. But they are self-preservers, fearing spiritual death by the sword. The human motto is, "live now, die later". We constantly put off the thought of death and don't realize that if we aren't living by the Spirit, we're already leading a dead life now, and headed to eternal death. Christ's solution is brilliant. His motto is, "die now, live forever". He died to break the power of death, and to set free all those who have lived their lives in fear of dying! (Hebrews 2:14–15)

By delivering us from the fear of death that we have because of our sin, Christ's solution is that we should go ahead and have a spiritual death by crucifying the flesh and severing the soul. Crucifying the flesh and severing the soul sets you free so you can live according to the Spirit—which leads to life and peace (Galatians 5:24, Luke 9:23, Romans 6:6). The obstacle that stands in the way, though, is a flesh and soul that intend to self-preserve.

> *Before you go through the enemy, you have to go through yourself first—because the enemy is hoping you stop yourself from going through with it!*

In that moment when I stood holding this sword before the very strongholds I intended to demolish, my soul and flesh surprised me when they cried out, "Please, don't hurt us!". I wanted to afflict the Devil, but I didn't want to afflict *myself*. Instead, I wanted to *cling* to my mindset, will, and emotions. My soul was attached to this stronghold of panic attacks and choking, because my emotions were still caught up in my past. Although my spirit told me to swing the sword, my soul was crying out in emotions that told me not to forgive God, not to let go of the accident, and to keep pouting so God would feel bad for me. I had the knowledge of the Lord in my hand, and I had His Word as my sword, but I couldn't go after that stronghold until I was willing to sever the connection between my soul and spirit. *I winced in pain at the sheer thought.* Sometimes it's the lies of the enemy that block our knowledge of God, but oftentimes it's the misguided self-preservation and stubbornness of our soul.

> *We are told to arrest every thought, take it captive, and make it obedient! Quit asking nicely and make an arrest in your soul.*

If you do not allow God's Word to separate your soul and spirit, your soul will not allow your spirit to swing that sword, because that sword comes for the soul first and foremost. Why is this? For example, if you struggle with sexual sin and pornography, there's no way you can swing the sword at the enemy until you swing it at yourself. Consider this thought, why have you clung to sex and porn (or anything else) for so long? Does it comfort you in hard times, does it distract you from a broken heart and loneliness, does it give you something to feel when you're totally numb in life? Or perhaps shame has driven you into isolation, so you don't know how to approach God in the secret place, so your bedroom has become a place of secrets to occupy your loneliness and darkness. (There is no condemnation for those who are in Christ, I speak this in love, so that His kindness may be a help to you! (Romans 8:1, Romans 2:4)).

When you feel yourself hesitate with the sword, there may be something your soul is attached to within that stronghold. The enemy has deceived you into desiring the stronghold. *Before you go through the enemy, you have to go through yourself first—because the enemy is hoping you stop yourself from going through with it!* We have to quit dealing with our flesh nicely. We are told to arrest every thought, take it captive, and make it obedient! Quit asking nicely and make an arrest in your soul.

When the Devil is able to set up a stronghold in our life, oftentimes this indicates there is an area of our soul that has agreed with the enemy over time, even passively, accidentally, or unknowingly. As you move forward, you need to be prepared to let the sword of the Spirit divide between your soul and spirit. It might not make sense why God would have you release bitterness, unforgiveness, anger, and hatred when someone hurts you. Hebrews 12:15 says that bitterness actually troubles you, and Ephesians 4:31 says these things grieve the Holy Spirit. We might not understand why it's so important to release some things that we feel are so valid to carry and defend. It's not always something our mind has the ability to comprehend, because the Bible explicitly tells us that God's thoughts and ways are higher than our own. So when we are clinging to our thoughts and our tendencies, please realize, we are living from a low place.

The Bible really does have our best interest in mind, spiritually, emotionally, and physically. Did you know that anger and hatred can lead to long term health problems? So can many other soulish tendencies, such as fear and anxiety. A mind set on what the flesh desires (sulking, carrying unforgiveness, defending hatred, clinging to worry, etc.) leads to death. But a mind set on what the Spirit desires (righteousness, the fruits of the Spirit, and unity in the Spirit, etc.) leads to life and peace (Romans 8:6). Thanks to scientific studies, there is much support for this biblical mental health principle. Having an unforgiving, worried, and troubled mind can lead to health complications and even premature death, while a peaceful mind leads to a healthier and longer life. Realize where this truth originated, in God's Word! He tells you what is good for you, even when you can't comprehend why forgiving someone would actually free *you*. Bondage leads to a life cut short, while freedom in Christ leads to a peaceful, long life. But we have to use God's Word as a sword, not as a crutch.

> *There should only be one stronghold over your life—and that is The Lord.*

Let Paul's words encourage you about self-crucifixion: "I want to know Christ—yes, to know the power of his resurrection and participation in his sufferings, becoming like him in his death, and so, somehow, attaining to the resurrection from the dead." (Philippians 3:10–11) When we die in Christ, He resurrects us to new life and power in Him. The "message of life" is so near to you, and prison break is at hand. A word of advice: the flesh is already dead, so don't try to live by it. Go ahead, bury the dead thing and be resurrected! There should only be one stronghold over your life—and that is The Lord (Psalm 27:1).

TACTICAL TRAINING

Drill In

Read: Hebrews 4:12

Reflect: When you feel yourself hesitating with the sword of the Spirit, there may be a part of that stronghold that your soul doesn't want to let go of. As you continue to identify the footholds and strongholds in your life, ask yourself, is there any reason you're unwilling to sever the tie? Is there any reason you're unwilling to crucify your flesh or demolish strongholds?

Read: Acts 5:17–41

Reflect: When the angel broke the disciples out of jail, they were instructed to preach "The Message of Life". When God breaks you out of bondage, He plans to use you. Do you know God's plans for you? How does He want you to use your story and freedom in Christ? Be still and ask Him.

Read: Romans 8:6–7

Reflect: Your mind sits at the intersection of your flesh and spirit. Although the spirit is willing to do the hard work, the flesh is weak. Those who focus on strengthening their mind to stay set on the Spirit are going to overcome the torments, tests, and temptations of the enemy and experience life and peace to the fullest.

How's your mind? How arrested are your thoughts, desires, and emotions? Can you think of any biblical means of strengthening your soul to stay set on the Spirit?

Drill Out

Don't let anything stand in the way of total freedom, not even yourself! Galatians 5:25 (KJV) says, "If we live in the Spirit, let us also walk in the Spirit." Pray this prayer, or one in your own words.

Holy Spirit, teach me how to live in the Spirit and walk in the Spirit at all times. Help me to take every thought captive and make it obedient to Christ (2 Corinthians 10:5). Help me to subdue my flesh so the Spirit can govern my mind with life and peace (Romans 8:5–6). I love You, Lord. I want Your living and active Word to be living and active in my life (Hebrews 4:12).

Drill Down

Hosea 4:6

Isaiah 55:8–11

Psalm 27:1

CHAPTER 7

The Shotgun Sniper

Six years into this fiasco, things were actually getting worse instead of better. I became desperate for freedom. I didn't want breathing exercises, coping mechanisms, or pills that took thirty minutes to kick in. More importantly, I did not want to accept that for the rest of my life I would be road kill to the fear, control, stress, anxiety, PTSD, panic attacks, choking, mental black outs, mental psychosis, voices, or demonic torments that hit me. I did not want anything short of what Jesus promised me, which is total freedom and authority! The Bible says believers have total authority over the enemy, and wherever the spirit of the Lord is, there is freedom.

I didn't want to read the Bible as lovely words on a page but having no real effect on my life. *I wanted God's living and active Word to be alive and active in my life!* I put my Bible on my desk one day, and I stared at it in fixed desperation. Then, I confessed out loud, "Either Your Word is true, or it's not. Either Your Word is all powerful, or it's not. *Either my weapons of warfare work, or they do not!*" Suddenly, I felt totally convinced that my biblical weapons of warfare could do exactly what they are said to do—*tear down strongholds.*

I was so embarrassed by the attacks. I'd been given the power of Christ as my inheritance, and somehow, somewhere along the way, I forfeited my rights. I didn't like to admit I was under the enemy's feet, but that's where I was after six years of being a pushover. I needed to regain the advantage.

One summer, I signed up for Mixed Martial Arts classes. I did this before heading to Uganda for a year to live as a missionary, then a single twenty-two-year-old female. I was moving to one of the most corrupt countries in the world, and there were very real safety concerns about me going alone. My support system agreed it was a good idea to take some classes for self-defense.

I want to discuss a mature matter for a moment, and I need you to enter into a mindset of purity and maturity. We are going to talk about the matter of being pinned down underneath the weight of an assailant. For some, this may be a triggering topic, and I invite you to skip over the following section between the asterisk heading (*).

✻

In self-defense classes, I expected to learn lots of punching maneuvers on my feet, but when the instructor learned I was going overseas for a whole year, alone, he sat me down in his office to have a serious conversation. He explained that most women who are attacked have to defend themselves when they are taken down to the ground. He told me about the "grappling" classes, which practice hand-to-hand combat on the floor. The goal is to regain the physical advantage after you've been put in a vulnerable position. Here's what I learned: *Once you are pinned down under your enemy, no amount of flailing will help you.*

This was a terrifying thought—once you are pinned to the ground, it is extremely difficult to escape. So much of a person's strength comes from standing on their feet and using their height and the momentum of a swinging arm. But when you are stuck underneath someone else, freeing yourself becomes difficult because you're crushed between the floor and the weight of your enemy. When you become boxed in, your movement is limited, and you are at a disadvantage.

I learned that if you come under attack, you should do whatever it takes to stay on top, because once you're under your enemy, it becomes much more difficult to resume the dominant position. It's not impossible, but it takes *strategy* to get back on top. My coach began to train me on grappling techniques. Instead of using force, I used strategic moves to flip my opponent's face into the ground.

※

The enemy is meant to be under our feet, not the other way around (Romans 16:20). The grappling classes taught me that when you're knocked to the ground, you need *strategic maneuvers.* I felt like I was being crushed under the weight of the Devil, and I knew I needed strategic maneuvers to regain the upper hand. I opened my Bible to 2 Corinthians 10:4 and I read that I have weapons of warfare to tear down strongholds. So I began to flip through the pages and search for every weapon I could find.

Though Paul mentions we have weapons of warfare, he never discloses what they are. I believe this was intentional on his part because our weapons look different from person to person and battle to battle. Suits of armor are tailored exactly to size, and the weapons must also befit the occasion. You don't bring a knife to a gun fight, and you don't fly water torpedoes in the air. Even video games teach this concept, giving you tips on which weapons work best for offense versus defense, which ones blow down specific barricades, and which weapons are most effective against specific villains.

It's interesting to me that Paul never wrote out a list of weapons though he is known to spell things out quite plainly. He listed out the armor of God (Ephesians 6:10–18), the offices of the church (Ephesians 4:11), and the gifts of the spirit (1 Corinthians 12:4–11), but when it comes to our weapons, he provides no such list. I believe this is because God fashions our weapons according to the person and according to the battle. Certain weapons are foundational (i.e., the name of Jesus, scripture, prayer, fasting, worship, etc.), while other weapons are tailored to size. The latter are provided by God, personalized for your situation, and supplied in your time of need. These types of weapons are usually provided with specific blueprints from Heaven and instructions to carry them out. Examples include writing and making decrees, conducting prophetic acts (like Jehoash and striking the arrows), and carrying out God's personalized instructions (such as walking around the walls of Jericho).

The six weapons I am about to introduce to you are not the only weapons we have; they are simply the ones I felt compelled to use in coordination with one another. Each of these I excavated from scripture and believe them to have a mighty purpose as a weapon of warfare. These are your weapons, but a lawyer might assert, "including but not limited to". You are not limited to these weapons; the Lord may supply you with others and that's okay.

When God began to take me into scripture to train me on my weapons of warfare, He used unique imagery to show me what these weapons could do. In prayer, I kept seeing a dynamic weapon that could blast ammo in all directions like a powerful shotgun and hit every bullseye with the accuracy of a sniper. I envisioned it every morning in prayer, so I eventually gave it a name, "The Shotgun Sniper". Simply put, it's our weapons of warfare loaded and fired at once—making one big *BOOM!*

Listed below are the six weapons we will be training in. If these are the weapons, I want you to consider the words leaving your mouth as bullets firing from a gun. In order to fire these weapons, your mouth must agree with God's Word and release the authority Christ gave you to overcome all the power of the evil one (Luke 10:19). Remember how video games educate the players about the use, power, and purpose of each weapon? Using scripture, I'm going to show you how powerful these six weapons are, and how to detonate them on the enemy.

As you learn about the mighty firepower they contain and the facets that make them uniquely able to demolish strongholds, you are going to feel *confident* as you step into your authority as a believer! Prepare to fire.

1. **Speak the WORD**
2. **Use the NAME**
3. **Plead the BLOOD**
4. **Remember through COMMUNION**
5. **Breakthrough with FASTING**
6. **Whoop in PRAYER**

TACTICAL TRAINING

Drill In

Jesus talked about the importance of having faith. In Matthew 17:20 He said that we can move obstacles as large as mountains when we speak to them in faith. If our faith can move mountains, imagine what it can do to strongholds! James 1:6 says, "But let him ask in faith, with no doubting, for the one who doubts is like a wave of the sea that is driven and tossed by the wind."

Fortify yourself in the Word so that you will not waver back and forth in doubt. If you truly believe what the Word of God has to say about your freedom and authority, then you won't put up with any nonsense from the enemy.

Fortify yourself by drilling in these powerful truths.

John 17:17 — God's Word is true!

2 Corinthians 10:4–6 — We have weapons of warfare to tear down strongholds!

2 Corinthians 3:17 — There is freedom where the Spirit of the Lord is!

John 14:17 — The Holy Spirit lives in you!

Mark 16:17 — The believer has authority to cast out demons!

Luke 10:19 — Christ has given you authority over all the power of the enemy!

Revelation 12:11 — The believer triumphs over the Devil!

John 8:36, Philippians 4:7, 2 Timothy 1:7, John 10:10 — The believer is meant to walk in freedom, peace, power, and life in abundance!

Drill Out

Spend some time in prayer with the Holy Spirit. Renew your mind with these scriptures, agree with God's Word, and meditate on the powerful truth and hope they speak for your life.

Drill Down

Romans 16:20

CHAPTER 8

Unsheathe the Sword

There is a huge difference between *being* something versus *being like* something. The Word of God is not *like* a sword, it *is* a sword. You can swing God's Word around *as* your sword. Take that in for a moment. You don't just read God's Word, you wield it. In Ephesians 6:17 Paul says the Word of God is a sword, the sword of the Spirit to be exact. In Revelation 19:15 John describes a corroborating vision he had, depicting Jesus with a sword coming out of His very mouth. This amazes me. Jesus didn't *carry* a sword, the sword is His own tongue, His own word, His own voice. God's Word *is* a sword. When you take His Word and wield it as your sword, you have a powerful weapon of warfare that is going to do some sick damage! This is what Hebrews 4:12 says about the written Word of God, "For the word of God is alive and active. Sharper than any double-edged sword..." With this resonating in me like great firepower, I started to view scripture as an armory! God's Word has weapons for us!

In English, we have one word for "word", which is simply "w-o-r-d". In Greek though, there are several versions and interpretations for "word" which are more specific. Two of these are *rhema* and *logos*. They are easy to differentiate. Rhema means utterance, or a spoken word; while logos means logic, word, or thought that embodies a message or idea.

Rhema is God's spoken word and logos is God's message written in the scriptures. One word you receive daily from the Holy Spirit, and the other word you receive daily from the Bible. These are two forms of how God speaks, and the difference between the two reveals to us something quite powerful that can change a life if weaponized.

Logos: Written Word

Hebrews 4:12

"For the word of God is alive and active. Sharper than any double-edged sword..."

Rhema: Spoken Word

Ephesians 6:17

"...the sword of the Spirit, which is the word of God."

There are two places in the Bible where the Word of God is likened to a sword. But each case is differentiated to be either God's written Word (logos) or spoken Word (rhema). In Hebrews 4:12 it says God's *written word* is *sharper* than any double-edged sword. The Greek word is *logos*, or the written word. In Ephesians 6:17 there's a slight twist. Paul also speaks of God's Word but uses rhema—God's *spoken word*. In one case, the written Word of God is described as being "sharper" than a sword. In the other case, the spoken Word of God *is* the sword. Why the discrepancy? Paul is making a progression. Imagine a sword being drawn from its sheath for use. While the written Word is *sharper* than any double-edged sword, it's the *spoken* Word that *is and becomes* the sword! Although the written Word (logos) is sharp, it is like a sword in a sheath. It has to be unsheathed to be weaponized.

> *Although the written Word (logos) is sharp, it is like a sword in a sheath. It has to be unsheathed to be weaponized.*

Let me show you an example of where the written Word was weaponized when someone took scripture and spoke it. In Matthew 4 we find Jesus in the wilderness where He fasted for 40 days and nights. The Bible is very clear at what point the Devil came to tempt Jesus. He didn't come at the beginning or middle of the fast when Jesus, in His humanity, was strong and at the prime of His mind and will. Instead, the Devil waited until Jesus was at His weakest. He came at the end of the fast when He was most vulnerable to temptation.

The Devil, also known as "the tempter", approaches Christ in the peak of His exhaustion and says, "If you are the Son of God, tell these stones to become bread." (Matthew 4:3). In other words, the Devil told Him, "Prove yourself. If you are the Son of God, provide for yourself. Show me a miraculous sign." Although a clever man, Jesus didn't reply with His own powerfully crafted thoughts, ideas, arguments, or rebuttals. Instead, He uses the most powerful weapon He has: God's Word. Jesus replies by quoting Deuteronomy 8:3, and when He does, He doesn't preach it with a new spin, He doesn't expand on its meaning or explain why Satan should back off, He simply quotes the scripture. Jesus says, "It is written: 'Man shall not live on bread alone, but on every word that comes from the mouth of God.'" (Matthew 4:4). As the scriptures roll off Jesus' tongue, God's Word becomes a sword by which the Son overcomes Satan. This is the power of God's Word; it is a powerful offensive weapon that delivers *quick* and mighty blows!

Notice how the Devil tempted Jesus three times. First, he tempted Jesus to make bread out of stones to satisfy His hunger. Second, the Devil tempted Him to prove Himself as the Son of God by jumping from the pinnacle and demonstrating an angelic rescue. Lastly, he tempted Christ to bow down and worship Satan in exchange for all the kingdoms of the world. The Devil was appealing to the basics of temptation, which are hedonism, egoism, and materialism. This is something that John later caught onto when he wrote 1 John 2:16. He categorized these temptations as the "lust of eyes" (materialism), "lust of body" (hedonism), and "pride of life" (egoism).

> *When we fall to the temptation of the flesh, we fall for the cheap shot.*

Earlier we visited how competitors study their opponents' signature moves. If we know their moves in advance, we know how to cut them off. In this vein, it's interesting to me that the Devil appealed first to the flesh. He is on to something. In fact, Matthew 26:41 gives no credit to the strength of our flesh, remarking, "The spirit is willing, but the flesh is weak." Because our flesh is so weak, the Devil often begins there. This is what caught my attention in Jesus' temptation. The Devil tempted His hunger first. It was a test of the flesh. The Devil knows our flesh is especially prone to weakness, so when he tempts us in our flesh, this is him low-balling us with the cheap shot. If a fighter goes into a wrestling ring and thinks there is a chance their opponent will fall with a simple blow to the knee, then they will attempt to spend just one minute trying to knock out the weak knee in hopes to end the match early. When we fall to the temptation of the flesh, we fall for the cheap shot. When this attempt failed, Satan had to switch tactics and take his efforts to the next level—*testing the aptitude of Christ's mind and spiritual understanding.*

In his second attempt, the Devil *himself* quoted scripture to Christ! Since Christ struck back with scripture, He set the tone for the battle and the enemy only had one choice: to use the same weapon to try and disarm Christ. Consider the old saying, "Don't bring a knife to a gunfight." If someone points a gun, you better have a gun to point back. The only way for Satan to counter-attack scripture was to join the duel with the same weapon. The tactical difference was that Satan used scripture to twist and distort the truth, hoping Jesus would fall for the trap. Satan chose to quote Psalm 91:11–12, hoping Christ would take the bait to prove scripture and do something foolish. Satan asserted, "If you are the Son of God, throw yourself down. *For it is written:* 'He will command his angels concerning you, and they will lift you up in their hands, so that you will not strike your foot against a stone.'" (Matthew 4:6). The Devil isn't afraid of the written Word, *he's studied it himself!* He has it memorized for his benefit! Here's the real danger. If *we* don't know the written Word, the Devil can twist it and deceive us.

When we pass the flesh test, the next level is the battlefield of the mind. There are Christians who didn't fall for the temptation of the flesh, but they listened to the enemy who manipulates and misguides scripture. A sly enemy will find a believer with zeal for the Lord and trick their zeal into opposing the move of God. Paul speaks of this group—rigid and religious, with misdirected enthusiasm, devotion, and passion. Of these people, he says, "I know what enthusiasm they have for God, but it is misdirected zeal. For they don't understand God's way of making people right with himself..." (Romans 10:2–3 [NLT]).

There are believers who have a pure lifestyle above reproach but the trap has succeeded to misguide their zeal, causing them to become so tight fisted that they are uncooperative to how God wants to move! When we know God's Word, we become cooperative to how the Holy Spirit is moving instead of trying to control something that is new to our experiences or beyond our understanding. If we pass the flesh test, we should stay humble and know the next level of attack is in the mind, oftentimes misdirecting a righteous person's zeal.

> *When we pass the flesh test, the next level is the battlefield of the mind.*

Attacking the mind takes a skilled approach, and it takes great Godly intelligence to defend against calculated deception. For this reason, we must spend much time in the written Word to know the scriptures, and much time in the presence of God to receive game changing revelation and understanding. This is the dynamic Jesus had! If Jesus was not grounded in the pure truth, the enemy could have surely won by using the very same weapon against Christ. So not only do we need to know the Word, but we also need to guard our understanding of the Word.

All that being said, notice that when Christ replied He didn't throw a scroll at the Devil and say, "Read this, it's my defense!" The written Word of God alone doesn't scare the Devil. Satan doesn't concern himself with Psalm 91 being on your screensaver or on the flashcard beside your bed. What he is afraid of is when scripture is embedded in your mind, poised to be unsheathed at any given moment. This is how God's Word becomes a sword—by how quickly you can unsheathe it and wield it. When you come face to face with an attacker, you don't have time to fumble around. You've probably seen a movie where a pistol duel took place. The most stressful scenes to watch are the old western versions in which the duel begins with holstered guns. In order to save your life, you have to be the fastest one to not only shoot, but to unholster.

When it's time to fight, you need to unsheathe *quickly*. And yet so many Christians fumble with the Word. When the Devil comes to steal, kill, and destroy, you don't want to be stuck trying to Google the Bible verse you need. You're stuck if you say, "Away from me, Satan, because I think it says somewhere in the Bible something along the lines of... hold on, I've almost got it..." You do not want to be a fumbler. When you draw a sword, you must draw it quickly.

The spoken Word (rhema) is referred to as a "quickened word", which is so characteristic of the sword of the Spirit. The rhema Word of God that is described as the sword of the Spirit in Ephesians 6:17 has to be *quick!* You must train in embedding scripture in your mind. You must memorize it, meditate on it, and practice recalling it, because it needs to come forth quickly. So how does it come forth? By the mouth. *We unsheathe it when we speak it.*

Remember, in Revelation 19:15 a sword came out of Jesus' mouth. Why would a sword be wielded in His mouth instead of His hand? When Paul describes the Word of God as a two-edged sword, he uses the Greek word "distomos" (Hebrews 4:12). When you break down this compound word, it comes from di (meaning two) and stomos (meaning one's mouth). *The two-edged sword is actually a "two-mouthed" sword.* When Jesus opposed the Devil He battled with scripture, saying, "It is written...". Christ unleashed God's Word from a second mouth— His mouth. Rick Renner writes,

> *First, that word came out of the mouth of God. Next, it came out of your mouth! When it came out of your mouth, it became a sharp, "two-edged" — or literally, a "two-mouthed" — sword. One edge of this sword came into existence when the Word initially proceeded <u>out of God's mouth</u>. The second edge of this sword was added when the Word of God proceeded out of <u>YOUR mouth</u>!*
>
> *The Word of God remains a one-bladed sword when it comes out of God's mouth and drops into your heart but is never released from your own mouth by faith. That supernatural word simply lies dormant in your heart, never becoming the two-edged sword God designed it to be.*
>
> *But something happens in the realm of the Spirit when you finally rise up and begin to speak forth that word. The moment it comes out of your mouth, a second edge is added to the blade! Nothing is more powerful than a word that comes first from God's mouth and then from your*

> *mouth. You and God have come into agreement, and that agreement releases His mighty power into the situation at hand!*[16]

This is how the Word becomes the double-mouthed or double-edged sword. We weaponize God's Word when we wield it from our mouth. If you never put scripture in your mouth, you're leaving a weapon on the table. Imagine a knife laying on the counter. You have a sharp object, but it will never become a weapon by just sitting there. You must pick it up and wield it, that's how it becomes weaponized!

Jesus knew what He was doing when He released scripture from His mouth to fight the Devil. He used the Word of God as a weapon, and it worked. When the Lord trained me for battle, He used imagery of modern weapons for rapid fire. I pictured Bible verses as bullets. When I studied scripture and embedded it in my mind, it was as if I was loading military-grade ammunition. And when I spoke scripture, I fired the weapon.

> **We weaponize God's Word when we wield it from our mouth.**

It's time for you to prepare your ammunition. The more rounds you have to fire, the better. In the *Tactical Training* following this chapter,

---

[16] Renner, Rick *You Have a Two-Edged Sword* (N.D), https://renner.org/article/you-have-a-two-edged-sword/.

you will be instructed to fill out sections one and two of ***The Shotgun Sniper Worksheet***. Your assignment is to identify your targets and load scriptural ammo. Since this is a critical step in your mission to tear down strongholds, let's discuss how to complete these two assignments prayerfully.

ASSIGNMENT #1 - IDENTIFY THE TARGETS

Begin by writing down every stronghold. If you aren't sure what your strongholds are, start with writing down everything in your life that is not a fruit of the Spirit, and everything that is not an attribute of freedom (Galatians 5:22–23). This will give you insight into any strongholds. If you are wrestling with whether or not something should be included, use scripture to sift the things you are unsure about. Freedom in Christ is straightforward, you are to be free indeed (John 8:36).

> *...where the Spirit of the Lord is, there is freedom.*
>
> *2 Corinthians 3:17*
>
> *I have given you authority to… overcome all the power of the enemy…*
>
> *Luke 10:19*
>
> *For God has not given us a spirit of fear, but of power and of love and of a sound mind.*
>
> *2 Timothy 1:7 (NKJV)*

I knew I wanted freedom from horrific things such as the debilitating panic attacks, choking, psychosis, and mental blacking out. But when it came to stress, worrying, and overthinking, I wondered if lesser weaknesses like these mattered. I used the scriptures above as my guide. As I considered the weaknesses and hindrances in my life, I asked myself, "Does this sound like freedom, authority, power, love, and a sound mind?" *If the answer was no, it had to go.*

In this exercise, you are identifying your targets. You'll want to track which targets you take out so you can move on to the next one, and the next one, until every target is eliminated by the power of Christ. In addition to listing all your targets, you will also want to fill out *Section Two*, where you will write down the scriptures you'll be using as ammunition to annihilate the enemy.

ASSIGNMENT #2 – LOAD YOUR AMMO

You will have great confidence standing your ground because you are standing on God's Word. For example, when I grew weary of praying for my freedom, I stood on Luke 18:7 which says, "And will not God bring about justice for his chosen ones, who cry out to him day and night? Will he keep putting them off?". Standing on this scripture as God's own Word, I trusted that if I kept crying out, He would not put me off, He would surely help me. I backed this up with the parable Jesus told in Luke 11, where a friend received what he requested based on sheer persistence and the audacity to ask for it. When I felt nervous about using God's Word as a weapon, and wondering if it could actually work, I stood on 2 Corinthians 10:4 which told me I have weapons of warfare that are mighty in God for pulling down strongholds. When I realized two of these weapons are God's own Word and the name of Jesus, I stood on Isaiah 55:11 which tells me God's Word accomplishes

His purpose and 2 Philippians 2:9–11 which says Jesus has the highest name and every knee will bow to the name of Jesus.

When I wondered if taking communion every day was a bust, I recalled Revelation 12:11 and used communion to remind me that I hurl down the enemy with the blood of the lamb (and the word of my testimony). When I doubted the impact of fasting and prayer, I stood on Mark 9:29, which tells me certain demons will only leave me with fasting and prayer. By the end of it all, I had pages of scripture that I was firing out of my mouth every single day. No matter how incompetent I felt throughout my worst days, scripture kept me on course with one mission on my mind: *if it's not freedom, it has to go.*

How do you know when the battle is done? Psalm 18:37–38 tells you when—it's not over until your enemy can't get back up! Leave no survivors.

I chased my enemies and caught them;

I did not stop until they were conquered.

I struck them down so they could not get up;

they fell beneath my feet. (Psalm 18:37–38 [NLT])

TACTICAL TRAINING

Drill In

Read: Revelation 19:15

Reflect: John had a vision of a sword coming out of Jesus' mouth. Why would a sword be wielded in Jesus' mouth instead of in His hand? Have you ever thought about wielding God's Word like a sword in your mouth?

Read: Hebrews 4:12, Ephesians 6:17

Reflect: While the written Word of God is sharper than any double-edged sword, the spoken Word is the actual sword! Yes, the written Word is sharp, but it is like a sword in a sheath. It has to be unsheathed to be weaponized. We bring forth the true power of the Word when we unsheathe it—speaking it out loud with confidence and conviction.

Read: John 8:36, 2 Corinthians 3:17

Reflect: Jesus died for us to be free, and this is a guarantee when we have the Holy Spirit. Use scripture as your guide to determine what needs to go. Ask yourself, "Does this sound like freedom, authority, power, love, and a sound mind?" If the answer is no, it has to go.

Drill Out

So far, we've been using drills to familiarize ourselves with our biblical weapons and tactics. Now, it's time to put it all together. You will find *The Shotgun Sniper Worksheet* at the back of the book. This is an all-in-one "hit list", weapon, and tactical manual. You will use this manual every day until you have the victory. Psalm 18:37–38 says, "I chased my enemies and caught them; I did not stop until they were conquered. I struck them down so they could not get up; they fell beneath my feet." Don't let up until the enemy can't get up. That's the plan.

Over the last few chapters, you've been identifying the strongholds in your life. Don't leave any outstanding warrants. It's time to make arrests and take captives. Turn to *The Shotgun Sniper Worksheet* and fill out Sections One and Two (revisit the information under Assignments 1 and 2 in the chapter if you need help).

Take your time and do this prayerfully. Remember, you cannot defeat an enemy you won't face, and you cannot exterminate your house unless you do it thoroughly, top to bottom, leaving no survivors. Be sure to ask the Holy Spirit to lead you as you identify your targets and load scriptural ammo to overcome the adversary.

Drill Down

Matthew 4:1-6

1 John 2:16

Matthew 26:41

Psalm 91:11–12

Romans 10:2–3

Deuteronomy 8:3

Psalm 91:11–12

Luke 18:7

Luke 11

2 Philippians 2:9–11

Mark 9:25–29

Psalm 18:35–38

CHAPTER 9

The Perfect Sacrifice

If someone gives up their life to save yours, it is for you to go on living, is it not? Say a friend takes a bullet for you, the reason they sacrificed their life is to save yours. How devastated would that friend be if you were to waste your life in bondage to oppression, depression, death, and destruction? Your friend would be devastated (not for themself, but for you). Jesus told His disciples, "Greater love has no one than this: to lay down one's life for one's friends." (John 15:13). When I read this, my story took a quick turn because of this one thought: if Jesus *died* so I could live and be set free, then I ought to live and be set free!

We have total victory because Jesus Christ (God in the flesh) gave His life for ours, demonstrating the greatest length love could go for a friend. Philippians 2:9–10 says, "Therefore God exalted him to the highest place and gave him the name that is above every name, that at the name of Jesus every knee should bow, in heaven and on earth and under the earth". The sacrifice of Jesus Christ is irreversible and insurmountable. You shall not die, but live, and declare the works of the Lord (Psalm 118:17). It is time for you to really live. It is time for you to be free indeed. Prepare your heart, for we are about to discover what victories and weapons we've been given through the love-sacrifice of Jesus Christ.

OUR NEED FOR CHRIST

Before we get to the cross, though, it is important to understand why we need Christ, and why He had to resort to extreme measures to purchase our lives with His own. The beginning is obvious: the fall of mankind. When Adam and Eve sinned, none of us stood a chance to even attempt restoring our right standing before the Lord. We discussed the detriment that is shame and guilt earlier in our conversation, concluding that shame drives us to hide from our Father. It wasn't God who broke fellowship with us, it was us who broke fellowship with Him. In this state of sin, God would not allow humanity to live forever. Adam and Eve could no longer eat of the tree of life, some believe because a loving God could not abandon His children to live for all of eternity with guilt and shame.

Fortunately for us, God's grace took over to pay for our redemption. *Since none of us could repair the relationship, God became one of us* (John 1:14, 1 Timothy 3:16, Hebrews 1:3)! Jesus became flesh and blood to destroy the Devil, who had the power of death (Hebrews 2:14–15). God became flesh, to do what we could not do: to make a way back to Him for us. (John 14:6, Hebrews 12:24). He did this through His very own blood.

> *Since none of us could repair the relationship, God became one of us! God became flesh, to do what we could not do: to make a way back to Him for us.*

Our lives had to be bought back, but why did it require such a high price? Why did Christ have to die? Again, John 15:13 tells us why. Christ spoke of the highest price love could possibly pay, to lay down your life for a friend's. Then, He told His disciples, "I no longer call you servants, because a servant does not know his master's business. Instead, I have called you friends, for everything that I learned from my Father I have made known to you." (John 15:15).

Are you making the connection? Jesus says we are His *friends*, and there is no greater love than to lay down one's life for a friend. God didn't repair our relationship through the cheapest expense possible. He didn't look at the repair quote and choose the easiest, most affordable option that would cost Him the least. Instead, He decided to display His love to us by paying the highest price possible. The author of life, the very essence and embodiment of love, decided to pay for our lives through the highest form of love there is. He laid down His life for ours.

Before He poured out His life, though, God allowed us to experience the repercussions of our free will used for sin. Have you ever noticed that sometimes we try to become like God without Him? This was actually what the whole debacle was with the forbidden fruit in the Garden of Eden. It wasn't the fruit that tempted Eve. An exotic fruit alone would hardly tempt anyone to sin against a God they personally knew, saw, walked with, spoke with, trusted, and so deeply loved. It was what eating of the fruit would grant Eve that tempted her. The Devil told her that to eat of the fruit would enlighten her to both good and evil. Eve knew what good was, but she had no idea what evil was.

A child has to learn every word for the first time, and whoever teaches the child that word, along with its meaning, context, and purpose has the great responsibility of teaching that child something that will shape their vocabulary, decision making, and worldview. Eve may not have known what evil was. We don't know if God explained evil to her since sin had yet to poison the world. When the serpent educated her about the knowledge of evil, he presented it as something to desire because it would make her like God. In Genesis 3:5, The Devil told her, "God knows that your eyes will be opened as soon as you eat it, and you will be like God, knowing both good and evil."

It's impossible to know what Eve's motive was at that moment, but if someone were to ask me, "Don't you want to be like God?", I would innocently think, "Absolutely! Oh, how that would please God so, for me to be more like Him!" When the serpent came to trick Eve, the temptation was, "Don't you want to be like God?". She may or may not have seen this as rebellion if her motive was to be more like the one she loved. In fact, Genesis 3:6 says Eve thought the fruit would give her *wisdom*. Wouldn't that please God—being more like Him in the fullness of wisdom? The problem is only God can make us like Him, and any attempt to become like God without God is *idolatry of the self*. Eve's mistake was not only a sin of disobedience of God's instruction, but it was also an idolatrous act of trying to be like God without God.

Today, we see that almost every religion in the world is convinced in some form that humanity can only attain heaven, eternity, improved reincarnation, nirvana, or "paradise" through the *self*. This striving of the self had begun immediately after the fall of man. We see humanity trying and trying through good deeds, self-righteousness, tenants, religious laws, and enlightenment to become worthy of their version of God's eternal presence. Many religions believe in God, but what they don't realize is that any pathway to God that is paved by efforts of the self insinuates that you are your own savior. Think about that. If you believe you can guarantee your salvation through religious law, self-righteousness, and good works, what you're really saying is that you don't need God, you can save yourself.

Christianity is the only exception. Christianity blows the lid off the pressure cooker—literally relieving us from the pressure we put on ourselves to become our own pathway and guarantee to God. The world says, "The way to God is through good deeds, religious laws, and self-righteousness". If this were true, every man would be condemned. Jesus says, "The way to God is through me, Christ. I am the way, the truth, and the life. No one comes to the Father except through me." (John 14:6). That's why the message of Jesus is called the Good News, every man can be saved.

After the fall, God already knew what humanity was going to do. He knew their shame would drive them away from God's grace and into self-works. It's as if God said to the Israelites, "I already know what y'all gonna' do. So let's get it out of your system. Put it to the test." We see throughout the entire Old Testament that God allowed us to try things our way—trying to be like God through our own efforts, and trying to save ourselves through works, self-righteousness, and religious laws. The purpose of the sacrificial and ceremonial rules in the Old Testament was to reveal to us God's holiness and the unrealistic standards it would take for us to approach Him by efforts instead of grace.

Have you ever read through Leviticus and wanted to pull your hair out at every teeny tiny, meticulous detail of how to offer a sacrifice? I admit, I've skipped chunks of Leviticus to save chunks of my hair. Imagine, though, not having the grace that we now have to skip through those meticulous portions of the Old Testament. Leviticus is primarily a rule book for how to offer sacrifices correctly, thereby cleansing man's sin before God. Millions of Jews had to uphold every single rule, but especially the priests, who had to oversee compliance down to the color of the tassels! If you were to say, "God, You put impossible demands on Your people!", you would be correct. If you were to say, "God, we are incapable of being perfect and blameless!", you would be correct. In fact, the Bible tells us, "None is righteous, no, not one." (Psalm 14:3, Romans 3:10).

If you read the Old Testament and think, "Yikes, this is drastic," God would agree. He never desired sacrifices, and He never desired a law that kills. In Psalm 51:16, the psalmist wrote, "You do not delight in sacrifice, or I would bring it; you do not take pleasure in burnt offerings." Hosea 6:6 declares, "For I desire mercy, and not sacrifice; and the knowledge of God more than burnt offerings." (NKJV). Christ reiterated this in Matthew 9:13 when He told His disciples, "But go and learn what this means: 'I desire mercy, not sacrifice.'" God used the Old Testament sacrifices to reveal to us something we need to know. We cannot become like God through efforts of our own. He does not desire that we approach Him through rituals and sacrifices but by the mercy of Christ. Hebrews 10 finally concludes that the sacrifices could never make us right with God, they only served as a shadow of the real thing that was coming—Christ!

In Galatians 3:22, Paul says God imprisoned everything under sin. God allowed us the experience of attempting to be perfect, blameless, and sinless, all to no avail. No one ever succeeded, and that unbearable law only resulted in death. The law was never meant to measure how close we could come to perfection in our own power. Paul resolves the purpose of the law was to reveal *our need for Christ* (Romans 7, Galatians 3)! Instead of realizing our need, though, we covered up our fallacy with even more striving to be like God through "works" and extra efforts of our own.

As an example, the Pharisees crushed people with unbearable religious demands (Matthew 23:4). They nitpicked themselves into perfection through outward actions and expected the same of everyone else. They were obsessed with becoming so righteous that they systemized God's Word into a rule book of behavioral and ceremonial dos and don'ts with disregard to the condition of the heart. In the end, they elevated their traditions over God's law, and Jesus rebuked them for that (Mark 7:9). This is idolatry of the self. It keeps us from accepting God's grace because we are living in this delusion that we can somehow measure up in our own power by trying harder. Trying to keep the law only ends in death, and this is God's point. We need Him to bring life. On that note, Jesus remarked, "The letter kills, but the Spirit gives life." We will spare ourselves much disappointment if we simply realize the only way to be like God is through God Himself. Not only could we never become pure and sinless like God without God, but we also cannot redeem ourselves with God without God. Every answer to our redemption with God is God Himself. We cannot pay for our errors. In that vein, even after the millions of sacrifices the Israelites had offered over the years, only one sacrifice could redeem them forever, and only one Lamb was worthy.

THE LAMB OF GOD

In order to redeem our lives, a price had to be paid. Leviticus 17:11 explains the price tag, "For the life of the flesh is in the blood, and I have given it to you upon the altar to make atonement for your souls; for it is the blood that makes atonement for the soul." (NKJV). Here, the Israelites were told by the creator of life where He placed life. He placed life in the blood, therefore, the way to atone for the soul is through the shedding of blood. Fortunately for us, God didn't ask for our blood on the altar (phew!). Instead, He allowed innocent animals to take our place, and little lambs often took center stage. What the Old Testament Jews didn't know at the time was that all of this was a prophetic foreshadowing of the real thing. When they had to offer repeated sacrifices again and again, and to shed the blood of countless animals, they genuinely believed they were experiencing the fullness of God's grace. But we know that God desired mercy and not sacrifice, and that this was only a *foreshadowing* of the good things to come (Hebrews 10:1).

The entire Old Testament sets the stage for Jesus Christ. Not only did the prophecies foretell the coming Messiah, but so did many of the events that took place. Jason Soroski is a Christian writer out of Missouri. In an article for Village Church, titled, *The Magnificent Truth in the Command "Do This in Remembrance of Me",* Jason writes, "Events in the Old Testament often serve the dual purpose of fulfilling God's promises to His people in the moment, while also providing a view of what is to come."[17] The Passover is the most symbolic in the foretelling of the sacrificial Lamb of God.

The Passover marks the dramatic exodus of the Israelites from a land where they were enslaved for over 400 years. On that last horrific night in Egypt, the Lord swept through the land and killed every firstborn son. As for the Israelites, the Lord gave them detailed instructions on how to mark their home so that the Lord would pass over them. This command would be repeated annually at the Passover dinner. Every year, the Israelites would choose a male lamb in its first year (a son!) and slaughter it without breaking a single bone and partake of it at dinner. They repeated this routine for nearly 2,000 years before Christ. The Israelites had no idea that all those years they were enacting the very sacrifice of Christ, our sacrificial Lamb, and the firstborn son of God who wasn't spared but given for our sake (Romans 8:32)!

Moving into the New Testament, we meet a man named John the Baptist who ministered daily to the public through a call to repentance and baptism. His life's mission was to prepare the way for the Messiah. As he was ministering in Bethany and baptizing folks on the shores of the Jordan River, Jesus stood out from the crowd. Christ walked toward John the Baptist, and in a mighty prophetic cry, *worlds suddenly collided!* The sin of the world, the Old Testament sacrifices, the Passover rituals, the prophecies of a savior and sacrificial lamb—they all sound off like magnificent fireworks when Christ emerges as the Word made flesh and the wilderness man bellows an announcement from the depths of his prophetic belly. Declaring the Messiah's arrival, John

---

17   Soroski, Jason *The Magnificent Truth in the Command "Do This in Remembrance of Me"* (July 19, 2020), https://www.biblestudytools.com/bible-study/topical-studies/the-magnificent-truth-in-the-command-do-this-in-remembrance-of-me.html

introduces Christ as, "The Lamb of God, who takes away the sin of the world!" (John 1:29).

Jesus was the spotless Lamb. He was the sinless sacrifice. When He prepared the disciples for His death, He told them, "The hour has come for the Son of Man to be glorified." It is no accident that Christ died during the Passover festival, along with all the other lambs. Nor was it a coincidence that the first communion took place at "The Last Supper", coinciding with the Passover meal so a final sacrifice could establish the New Covenant (Hebrews 10:9).

Nearly 2,000 years prior, hundreds of thousands of lambs were sacrificed to protect the lives of the Israelites and deliver them out of slavery. 2,000 years later, Christ sat around the Passover meal with the "ones God gave him" and He remembered God's great faithfulness to His people. Like every other Passover meal He had ever participated in, Christ proceeded to pass each cup in sequence according to the ceremonial procedures. The disciples may have been surprised, then, when Christ concluded the ritual they had all strictly followed since they were little boys by introducing a new tradition. Unlike any year before, Jesus took a loaf of bread and broke it. Giving it to His disciples, He told them, "This is my body, which is given for you. Do this in remembrance of me." Then, passing the wine, He told them, "This cup is the new covenant between God and His people—an agreement confirmed with my blood. Do this in remembrance of me as often as you drink it." (1 Corinthians 11:24–25 [NLT]).

The next morning, His body was given, and His blood was poured out, exactly as enacted. The long-awaited sacrificial Lamb had been slain. While most crucifixions had to be quickened by breaking the person's legs, Jesus died ahead of the others. To make sure He was dead, the guards pierced His side with a spear. When it came time to speed up the death of the two thieves by breaking the bones in their legs, they left Christ's slain body alone. Just like the Passover lambs, His bones were not broken. This fulfills what was prophesied. Later, John ensured people made the connection, explaining, "These things happened so that the scripture would be fulfilled: 'Not one of his bones will be broken.'" (John 19:36). He was testifying to the fulfillment of what the psalmist prophesied, "He protects all his bones, not one of them will be broken." (Psalm 34:20). Every detail of the Old Testament sacrifices, the Passover events, and the Messianic prophecies were all a foretelling of the price the Messiah would pay. It is just as John the Baptist announced. *Christ is our sacrificial Lamb of God.*

Passing the wine, Jesus said, "This is the new covenant between God and his people, an agreement confirmed with *my blood*." When Christ came into the world, He set aside the first covenant to establish the second, concluding that the Old Testament law was only a foreshadowing of the real thing—God's love poured out for us. Because of His love for us, His friends, God paid for our lives through the highest price there is. *His life*.

Take a moment to read Hebrews 10:1–18 and reflect on what God did for your sake:

> *The law is only a shadow of the good things that are coming—not the realities themselves. For this reason it can never, by the same sacrifices repeated endlessly year after year, make perfect those who draw near to worship. 2 Otherwise, would they not have stopped being offered? For the worshipers would have been cleansed once for all, and*

would no longer have felt guilty for their sins. 3 But those sacrifices are an annual reminder of sins. It is impossible for the blood of bulls and goats to take away sins.

Therefore, when Christ came into the world, he said:

"Sacrifice and offering you did not desire,

but a body you prepared for me;

with burnt offerings and sin offerings

you were not pleased.

Then I said, 'Here I am—it is written about me in the scroll—

I have come to do your will, my God.'"

First he said, "Sacrifices and offerings, burnt offerings and sin offerings you did not desire, nor were you pleased with them"—though they were offered in accordance with the law. 9 Then he said, "Here I am, I have come to do your will." He sets aside the first to establish the second. 10 And by that will, we have been made holy through the sacrifice of the body of Jesus Christ once for all.

Day after day every priest stands and performs his religious duties; again and again he offers the same sacrifices, which can never take away sins. But when this priest had offered for all time one sacrifice for sins, he sat down at the right hand of God, 13 and since that time he waits for his enemies to be made his footstool. For by one sacrifice he has made perfect forever those who are being made holy.

The Holy Spirit also testifies to us about this. First he says:

"This is the covenant I will make with them

after that time, says the Lord.

I will put my laws in their hearts,

and I will write them on their minds."

Then he adds:

"Their sins and lawless acts

I will remember no more."

And where these have been forgiven, sacrifice for sin is no longer necessary.

(Hebrews 10:1–18, [NIV])

INTIMIDATION IS POWERLESS

When it clicked for me that Christ died so I could live in Him and be free, it felt as if someone poured ice cold water over me. I was awakened! I wondered how I could miss the picture for so long. For six years I was being beat down by deep and crippling bondage. This bondage stole my breath, my voice, my peace, my time, my boldness, and it beat me down by extreme intimidation. I thought I was powerless against this bondage and that's why I lived with it quietly for six years. It wasn't until I read Galatians 5:1 that I knew something was wrong according to the sacrifice that was paid for me. Paul explains, "It is for freedom that Christ has set us free. Stand firm, then, and do not let yourselves be burdened again by a yoke of slavery."

I finally realized all of my bondage only ever succeeded by *intimidation*. The choking issue had gotten so bad that I had one of my pastors pray over me. She listened to me explain how my PTSD kept getting worse even six years later, evolving into choking and breathing issues that terrified me. Pastor Michelle Passey listened to the Holy Spirit for a moment, then told me, "It's just smoke and mirrors." Suddenly, I realized I was living in delusion about my freedom and power. If Christ set me free, then I was to be free! *Period.* And if God said to never become a slave to anything ever again, then by golly, anything that tried to chain me, block me, or hinder me was about to go *boom!*

The delusion was exposed. Here's the thing about intimidation. If the enemy actually had real power over you, he wouldn't need intimidation. You are the one who wields the power of Christ in you, and the only way the enemy can get you to become a slave is by convincing you that you're powerless! It's all a ruse. This "smoke and mirrors" strategy causes the enemy to appear bigger, more powerful, and more dominant than he really is. Consider *The Wizard of Oz* and the man behind the curtain. He was no wizard at all, he was a conman and liar. Because he had no real power, he had to hide behind a curtain and use tricks to make people cower and fear him. While he didn't have any real power, he became powerful through trickery and intimidation.

Let me be clear; I don't want you to think the enemy is not a threat. He is still a thief, killer, and destroyer (John 10:10). I just want to put into perspective how silly it is for us to cower in the face of intimidation, because we are the ones who have the power of Christ in us! Christ died to set you free from every form of slavery, and through Him, He gave you power and authority to overcome the enemy (Luke 10:19). This is not an empty promise, it is a guarantee. You don't have to beg for something that is guaranteed. John 8:36 puts it this way, "So if the Son sets you free, you will be free indeed."

THE TRIPLE THREAT

Before Jesus offered Himself as the sacrificial Lamb of God, He announced His death in a peculiar way. He said, "The hour has come for the Son of Man to be glorified." (John 12:23). The book of Philippians tells us that Christ humbled Himself unto human likeness so an immortal God could die for us, offering His life for ours. Hebrews 2:15 says His death *broke* the power of the Devil, the one who once held the power of death! This is how He freed us. Because of His sacrifice for us, Christ was exalted to the highest place, given the highest name, and *glorified*. He was glorified because of His sacrifice, and in His glory, we were given extraordinary weapons and tactics. Because of His *body* that was given, His *blood* that was shed, and His *name* that was exalted, we have mighty weapons and tactics that make strongholds go *BOOM!*.

I call this trio—the name, blood, and body of Jesus—the "triple threat", and I want to empower you with three tactics to enforce Christ's victory in your life.

Command Your Rights — Use the Name

For the first part of the triple threat, we have the mighty name of Jesus. Imagine being handed a badge that demands immediate compliance and submission. It does not matter where you go or what you encounter, this badge trumps every adversary in any jurisdiction. In Luke chapter 10, Jesus appointed seventy-two followers to go ahead of Him into the towns and places He was about to go through. Dispersing themselves in all directions, each team encountered diverse territories and varying demonic manifestations. In other words, everyone had a different experience, and yet the groups came back with the same report! After preparing the way, the seventy-two came back overjoyed about what they had seen! Excited, they returned to Jesus and reported, "Lord, even the demons submit to us *in your name."* Christ told them, "I saw Satan fall like lightning!" How proud He must have been when His disciples boldly stepped out and used the badge they were given. Then, He said, "I have given you authority to trample on snakes and scorpions and to overcome all the power of the enemy..." (Luke 10:19).

When Christ was on earth, the power to use His name was limited to the followers He chose to give the authority to. In this case, it was the seventy-two. Today, though, the group is no longer a select few. Just before Christ ascended into Heaven, He explained the qualifications for who could use His name—*anyone who believes.* He announced, "And these signs shall follow them that believe; In my name shall they cast out devils..." (Mark 16:17 [KJV]). According to Jesus, anyone who believes in Christ can use His name to cast out devils, and this is a sign that naturally follows believers.

Names carry power when they are tied to a person of authority. Pause and contemplate what Paul says about how God exalted Christ because of His sacrifice for us, and what happened to His *name.* Philippians 2:8–11 reads,

> *And being found in appearance as a man, he humbled himself by becoming obedient to death— even death on a cross! Therefore God exalted him to the highest place and gave him the name that is above every name, that at the*

> name of Jesus every knee should bow, in heaven and on earth and under the earth, and every tongue acknowledge that Jesus Christ is Lord, to the glory of God the Father.

When the Philippians read Paul's letter and believed that Jesus owns the highest name, this registered to them as something they could use *against* the enemy. These people were accustomed to messengers and representatives who could travel across far lands carrying *only* the name of their king, dignitary, or commander. They could say to someone, "Do this", and if they said it in the name of the ruler, this was a direct command which carried great authority. Jesus has the *highest* name. When you speak His name, there is no other creature in Heaven above or earth below who has a superior name to combat the authority you assert when you use His name. *So, use it.* The disciples sure did!

You can use His name as a weapon and eviction notice. Although it's a pre-Christ reference, my favorite example of a person using God's name as a weapon is David. When the young shepherd boy took his stand against Goliath, he told the giant, "You come against me with sword and spear and javelin, but I come against you in the name of the Lord Almighty, the God of the armies of Israel, whom you have defied." (1 Samuel 17:45). You've probably played the game "Rock Paper Scissors" in which the goal is to upstage your opponent with the superior weapon. Well, David faced a real life version of "Sword Spear Javelin", and while I'm not familiar with ancient Philistine weapons, they sound pretty gnarly.

So how did this unlikely duel come about? The Israelites and Philistines were positioned for a bloody war. Instead of losing so many men on both sides, though, they agreed to a single combat. In this settlement, each side would send one champion to represent their nation in a battle to the death. 1 Samuel 17:16 says Goliath came forward every morning and every evening for 40 days to take his stand for single combat. That's eighty invitations for an opponent to step forward, yet Saul, the militant leader and king over Israel, hid cowardly in the camp. David, though, came to the battlefield one day merely to deliver food to his brothers. He soon found himself fulfilling a greater assignment. While Saul hid at eighty invitations for combat, David approached the giant almost as soon as he arrived. In this story, it's quite apparent who the underdog was. When a skinny shepherd boy volunteers to duel a jurassic-sized champion in a battle to the death, all bets were on Goliath. Afraid for David, the king offered his own armor for protection. David respectfully declined. The lad insisted he enter combat in shepherding clothes as his armor and a slingshot as his only weapon. While it's true he knocked out the giant with a stone and good aim, the true weapon is often overlooked in the story—it was the one he announced. David's primary weapon was never a slingshot and stone… *His primary weapon was the name of the Lord.*

Here's the connection I want you to make. The only way a slingshot and stone stand a chance against superior weapons and a trained killer is if that stone hits the *bullseye* in one shot. That's the only way. In fact, no matter what champion or weapon Israel sent out, not a single Israelite warrior stood a chance to survive the battle against the towering Goliath. Whoever approached this giant had one shot to hit the enemy in the bullseye, because if the battle resorted to a tango, it would be the end for Israel. Although David walked onto the field with a slingshot, he never announced it as his weapon. He mentioned something else, something *higher*. When the Philistine came against David with a sword, spear, and javelin, David didn't say, "I come against you with my DIY slingshot and the little stone I just cleaned off from the stream." Actually, he said, *"I come against you in the name of the Lord almighty."* This was his primary weapon, and the very reason that stone hit the bullseye in one shot! This is the power of His *name*! His name hits the bullseye every time.

His name is superior to every giant. It is by the name of Jesus that we are saved (Acts 4:12, Romans 10:13). We are washed, sanctified, and justified by His name (1 Corinthians 6:11). Demons flee at the sound of His name (Luke 10:17). Sickness and disease are healed to perfect health in His name (Acts 3:6, 3:16, Mark 16:18). His name can subdue and destroy every giant in your life. We have been given His name to do the same works He did, to use His authority in all matters, and to enforce the victory of the cross (John 14:13–14)! Right now, there are things in your life that need to bow to the name of Jesus. This is a name-drop that will make demons flee, so flex your authority in Christ-glorified and say, "In the name of Jesus, detach from me!".

> *We have been given His name to do the same works He did, to use His authority in all matters, and to enforce the victory of the cross.*

Enforce Your Rights — Plead The Blood

Second in the triple threat, we have the blood of Jesus. My heart was wrenched out of my chest when I learned there are Christians convincing other Christians that we are not supposed to be caught up on the blood of Jesus. I have another name for these types, "Queasy

Christians". Queasy Christians say we are not supposed to think of the blood, speak of the blood, or dwell on the blood. I was especially shocked by a blogger who assured his readers that the Gospels (the books which were written with one reason: to prove the death and resurrection of Christ both historically and supernaturally) barely speak of the crucifixion. The blogger also asserted that the blood and sacrifice of Jesus is mostly absent from the New Testament topics. In this vein, the blogger proposed that we should not dwell on the blood of Christ by dramatizing the crucifixion now that it's over. Dear reader, I beseech you to run far, far away from Queasy Christians. Jesus did not pay for your life with gold and silver because such things lose their value. He paid with something priceless, so do not let the blood of Jesus lose its value in your life, for there is no redemption for you without the blood of Jesus (Ephesians 1:7, 1 Peter 1:18–19).

From Genesis to Revelation, blood has been speaking. In Genesis 4:10 we find Abel has been murdered, and God says to the elder brother, "Your brother's blood is crying out to me from the ground!". This man's blood was taken, but another was given. Hebrews 12:24 says that Jesus' blood, "speaks a better word than the blood of Abel". Blood has been crying out since the beginning of mankind, speaking to God about the evil of our sins. But when Christ's blood was shed, He spoke of forgiveness and redemption, saying, "Lord, forgive them, for they know not what they do", and "It is finished" (Luke 23:34, John 19:30). By saying, "It is finished", Jesus turned a page with His life by setting aside the first covenant to establish the second (Hebrews 10:9). I encourage you to pause and read through Hebrews, chapters nine and ten. For anyone who is on the fence about the mention of blood, the book of Hebrews gives a good look at the spilled blood of Jesus Christ. Hebrews 9:12 says, "He did not enter by means of the blood of goats and calves; but he entered the Most Holy Place once for all by his own blood, thus obtaining eternal redemption." He did this to do away with sins and sacrifices, and by this new covenant, we have been made holy through the sacrifice of the body of Jesus Christ once for all (Hebrews 9:26, 10:10).

I am flabbergasted by believers who claim the Bible barely mentions the blood and hushes believers into queasy silence. If we are not meant to dwell on the blood beyond the resurrection, then tell me why Jesus was willing to lose followers on a daring statement that they must eat His body and drink His blood to have eternal life (John 6:60, 6:66). Jesus told His disciples, "Very truly I tell you, unless you eat the flesh of the Son of Man and drink his blood, you have no life in you." (John 6:53). How quickly does a person die once they begin to lose blood? It can be a matter of seconds to minutes. Life is in the blood, and Jesus was forecasting not a cannibalistic practice, but one of precious remembrance. He lost a slew of followers after this statement, but if they had not been so queasy of the mention, they would have soon realized Jesus was speaking of bread and wine, a communion to remember His sacrifice.

I submit to you, if we are not supposed to dwell on the blood, why did Jesus say we should remember Him *every time* we drink wine (1 Corinthians 11:25)? If we are not meant to dwell on the blood after Christ's resurrection, then why is the Worthy Lamb in the Throne Room of Heaven—before the sight of God Almighty—*still stained by the blood* (Revelation 5)? I can tell you why. Because the Father and Son have not forgotten the precious blood. In fact, when Christ instructed His disciples to take communion, He told them He would not drink wine again until the day we are all in Heaven (Matthew 26:29). Jesus is still thinking about the blood, and He's waiting to remember it together with you in Heaven.

Invoke Protection

The blood of Christ is the New Covenant. This New Covenant is our inheritance, it's God's promise of redemption and salvation to us through Christ. Here's the thing about inheritance, though, anyone who wants to steal from you will test you, hoping you don't know what's due to you by inheritance. The same goes with lawsuits. A courtroom shark will hope you don't know your rights.

You've probably heard the phrase, "I plead the Fifth". When a person pleads their Fifth Amendment, they're invoking protection that is afforded to U.S. citizens through the Bill of Rights. *Pleading a right invokes protection.* The protection is rightfully yours, but verbally invoking that protection stops anyone who is trying to manipulate you, overstep you, or cheat you. If a person is unfamiliar with the law, they might not know they can plead certain rights to enforce protection. A person who doesn't know about the powerful rights afforded to them is clueless and unprotected, prone to the manipulation of cross-examiners, because they don't know how to call on their rights. When a person pleads an Amendment, they demonstrate they know their rights and they intend on exercising them, using them to their full defense.

You have a right to enforce every victory in your life by the name and blood of Jesus! You might be asking, "If my rights have already been paid for by Christ, why would I have to 'plead' for them?" To "plead" the blood of Jesus does not refer to an emotional appeal or begging. "Plead" in this case means to invoke. In the same way we can plead a right to enforce our freedoms, we can also plead the blood of Jesus to do the same spiritually. This practice is for your benefit. Similar to taking communion, this practice brings you into powerful agreement of what Christ's sacrifice did for you. He died for you to have *total freedom* in your salvation through Him! When you plead the blood of Christ, you will enforce your rights to freedom by using the blood of Christ as your defense! This is a powerful practice that will keep you standing firm against any lie from the enemy that you're not truly free. Plead the blood and shut him up.

To plead the blood of Christ is not a doctrinal practice, nor is an occurrence found in the Bible, nor should it be a matter of division. We get to apply wisdom and inspiration from the Holy Spirit and decide how we use prayer to agree with God's Word. Pleading the blood is one way we can do that. It is a powerful agreement with what the Word of God says about the blood of Christ. When I struggled with a battle in my mind, whether that be sin or panic attacks, Hebrews 9:14 told me that the power of Christ's blood could cleanse my conscience so that I could serve the living God! 1 John 1:7 tells us the blood of Jesus can purify us from any sin that we struggle with. Isaiah 53:5 says we've been healed by His stripes (the blood that spilled forth when He was beaten and flogged). We are afforded certain rights through Christ's blood, including a cleansed mind, holiness, freedom, and healing. When the enemy comes to steal, kill and destroy, all we must do is enforce our blood rights!

Don't You Dare Plead The Thorn

Cross-examination is defined as, "The formal interrogation of a witness called by the other party in a court of law to challenge or extend testimony already given."[18] We must each take the stand to give our own testimony about Jesus. Paul straightened this out when he told the Jews that no one can inherit salvation through the faith of their lineage and those who served God before them. Each and every one of us must take the stand. You might have a compelling testimony rehearsed, but will it stand up against cross-examination? The cross-examiner's job is to prove you guilty, so they hound you relentlessly in an attempt to poke holes in your testimony. A person who is guilty might choose to plead the Fifth Amendment, and by doing so they refuse to answer a question that might incriminate them.

Satan is called "the accuser of the brethren" (Revelation 12:10). When you want to beat the hold that pornography has over you, he will begin by convincing you how powerful that sin is. He'll remind you, "That addiction has had you bound since you were ten years old. Now you're 25 and bringing pornography into marriage." Then, like he always does, he's going to twist scripture to see if you know your rights. He'll say, "I see that you claim Galatians 5:1 as your defense, that Christ died to set you free and that you should no longer be a slave. You've also claimed Romans 6:7 as your defense, which says that Christ died to set you free from the power of sin." Satan twists scripture to see if you'll forgo your blood rights. He wants you to take the easy way out, so he'll say, "But everyone has a thorn in their flesh. This is yours. *What plead you?*". Don't incriminate yourself. *When Christ wants you to plead the blood as your defense, do not plead the thorn!*

Regarding the thorn in the flesh, notice how Paul explains the thorn kept him humble. Let's read it directly, "So to keep me from becom-

---

[18]   https://www.merriam-webster.com/dictionary/cross-examination

ing proud, I was given a thorn in my flesh, a messenger from Satan to torment me and keep me from becoming proud." (2 Corinthians 12:7 [NLT]). I've heard people describe lust, pornography, or addiction as the "thorn in the flesh" that God won't remove from them. I want to clear up any confusion. God left the thorn alone to keep Paul humble, not to keep Paul in sin. God told Paul it was in his best interest to leave the thorn alone. Why? Because Paul was at risk of becoming too proud because of all the great revelations he received. We know that God opposes the proud and shows favor to the humble (James 4:6, Proverbs 3:34). God humbled Paul so He could favor Paul. 2 Corinthians 12:9 does not say, "My grace is sufficient for you, for My strength is made perfect in sin." No, it says "for My strength is made perfect in weakness." We've got to stop claiming sin as a thorn in our flesh.

> **When Christ wants you to plead the blood as your defense, do not plead the thorn!**

When God refused to remove Paul's thorn, He didn't condemn Paul to a lifetime of compulsive sin. That would contradict what God was teaching the Roman church *through* Paul—we don't excuse sin because of grace (Romans 6:1–2). The way you know whether you should remove a thorn or leave it is by talking to a doctor. Perhaps the thorn for Moses was his trouble with speaking, but it was certainly not disobedience (Exodus 4:10–11, Numbers 20:6–12). While God uses a weakness to perfect His power in us, He will not use sin to do the same.

Don't plead sin as the thorn in your flesh when the blood of Christ has set you free!

Revelation 12:11 tells us we overcome Satan by the blood of the Lamb and the word of our *testimony*. Notice the combo. When we speak Jesus' blood aloud, we can actually use His blood *as* our testimony. Against sin and addiction, say this, "The precious blood of Christ has cleansed my conscience from acts that lead to death so I can serve the living God!" (1 Peter 1:19). Against your past, say this, "The blood of Jesus purifies me from all sin!" (1 John 1:7). Against shame, say this, "I am justified, the blood of Jesus draws me to boldly enter God's most holy presence!" (Hebrews 10:19, Romans 5:9). Against striving and works, say this, "The blood of Jesus has redeemed me from the empty way of life!" (1 Peter 1:18). Against the fear of death and damnation, say, "The blood of Christ gives me eternal life with my Beloved Lamb!" (John 6:55–59). Against self-condemnation, say, "He bore my transgressions so I can be redeemed!". Against disease, say, "By His stripes I am healed!" (Isaiah 53:5, 1 Peter 2:24). Against weakness and sickness, say, "I remember what Christ's body and blood did for me!" (1 Corinthians 11:24–30).

When the Devil comes to destroy you, testify about the blood. Make *him* queasy.

> ***While God uses a weakness to perfect His power in us, He will not use sin to do the same.***

Remember Your Rights — Partake in Communion

The third tactic to enforce your rights through Christ's glorification is by taking communion. Luke 22:19–20 shows Christ leading His disciples through the first communion; "And he took bread, gave thanks and broke it, and gave it to them, saying, 'This is my body given for you; do this in remembrance of me.' In the same way, after the supper he took the cup, saying, 'This cup is the new covenant in my blood, which is poured out for you.'" I took Christ's words to heart when He said to remember Him through communion, so I implemented communion into my warfare strategy. I did not see communion as an offensive weapon to use against the enemy, actually, I realized it's a defense to fortify the believer. Communion is for *us*. It benefits us. (Just as taking communion improperly *harms* us.)

Taking communion doesn't cause you to remember in the same sense that we remember a memory. A memory is in the past, but remembrance transcends into the present. On the Fourth of July and Juneteenth, we remember how others made sacrifices for the freedoms we have today. *Remembrance is not a flashback to the past, it's a flashforward to how the past is still impacting our present.* Taking communion reminds us that someone in the past paid for the price of our freedom so we can live free today. The past enforces a victory in the present even 2,000+ years later. When you take communion, you remember Jesus died to set you free from slavery. You remember His body was given for you. You remember His blood was shed to purchase your life. As you recall all of this, you renew your mind to agree with the victory of Christ's sacrifice for you.

Communion can make or break your health, vitality, and freedom. 1 Corinthians 11:29–32 might explain why we have so many Christians who are weak, sick, and have spiritually fallen asleep. There is a judgment if you partake of Christ's body and blood in an unworthy manner. While we don't need to panic about judgment or overthink it every time we take communion, we do need to have a healthy fear and reverence when taking communion. Paul puts it like this, "Examine yourself". As simple as that. He explains, "So then, whoever eats the bread or drinks the cup of the Lord in an unworthy manner will be guilty of sinning against the body and blood of the Lord." (1 Corinthians 11:27). Examples of taking communion unworthily are feasting on the communal wine and becoming drunk, pigging out on the holy bread as if it were an appetizer, partaking with unrepented sin, and failing to "recognize the body". In other words, displaying irreverence or indifference over something Holy that represents the body and blood of Christ.

When you take communion unworthily, you sin against the body and blood of Jesus, and it actually brings a judgment on *your* body and blood. Verse 30 says, "That is why many among you are weak and sick, and a number of you have fallen asleep". This might explain how we have so many sick, weak and sleeping believers! How many Christians have weakened the message of the blood and have since fallen weak? How many Christians have spoken ill of the blood and have since fallen ill? How many Christians have slept on the blood and since fallen asleep? When you sin against the body and blood of Jesus, you eat and drink judgment on yourself (1 Corinthians 11:29). I propose to you that one such unworthy manner of dangerous implications is partaking in "Communion Sundays" but silencing the mention of blood in the sermons and worship sets, as the queasy ones do. Woe to you.

One of my mentees once told me that a church lady told her not to speak of the blood or plead the blood of Jesus in prayer. I told her if she wants to stay oppressed, then she should take that kind of advice.

But if she wants to be freed, she should meditate on every single victory that we are handed through the body and blood sacrifice of Jesus Christ and do whatever it takes to experience the complete transformation of a holy blood transfusion.

When I needed freedom, I implemented daily communion into my prayer strategy. Taking communion every day was a great defense to me. I often felt a wavering stir within me to give up my fight, but when I began to partake in communion, it was the act of *remembrance* that anchored me. *Remembrance* armed me with a promise of freedom that was indisputable and a determination that could not be knocked down. This remembrance motivated me to continue contending for my freedom until it matched the promise of "life in abundance" (John 10:10).

So, what plead you? Are you going to let the Devil push you around, or are you going to plead your blood rights? You have a triple threat to use as your defense. Speak His all-powerful name, plead His victorious blood, and stand firm by remembering what His sacrifice bought for you— Your salvation and freedom in Christ! Go ahead, enforce the victory of the cross and testify about the power of Christ.

Command Your Rights
(Use the Name)

Enforce Your Rights
(Plead the Blood)

Remember Your Rights
(Partake in Communion)

TACTICAL TRAINING

Drill In

Read: Philippians 2:8–11, Mark 16:17, 1 Samuel 17:45, Luke 10:17, 1 Corinthians 6:11, John 14:13–14

Reflect: Don't take no for an answer. Command your rights by speaking the name of Jesus. Is this something you have been doing already? If not, how will you start commanding your rights?

Read: Ephesians 1:7, 1 Peter 1:18–19, 1 John 1:7, Romans 5:9, Hebrews 12:24, Hebrews 9:1–28, Hebrews 10:1–22, Revelation 12:11

Reflect: Have you ever experienced the Devil working to steal, kill, and destroy in your life? What does the blood of Jesus do for you, what does it speak over your life? The next time the enemy tries to cheat you from your God-given rights as a believer, enforce your rights by pleading the blood.

Read: Luke 22:14–20, John 6:53–59, Isaiah 53:5, 1 Peter 2:24, 1 Corinthians 11:23–30

Reflect: Forgetfulness can cause us to lose valuable things. When we are forgetful of Christ's sacrifice, we misplace the treasures of the believer, such as our identity, the understanding of our redemption, and our authority as heirs. This is why Christ instructed us to remember. Remember your rights by partaking in communion.

Drill Out

Find something to serve as the communion elements (i.e., wine and bread, or juice and crackers, etc.) and turn to the section in the Appendix titled, ***How to Take Communion***. Do this in remembrance of Jesus Christ, the Lamb who is worthy. Reflect on the perfect sacrifice that bought your redemption and freedom in Christ.

Drill Down

This chapter was filled with important scriptures, so the list is pretty long. The next chapter doesn't have so many, so feel free to spread them out, if that's the way the Spirit leads you.

John 15:13–15	Psalm 34:20
Psalm 118:17	Romans 3:10
John 1:14, John 1:29	Hosea 6:6
1 Timothy 3:16	Matthew 9:13
Hebrews 1:3	Galatians 3:22
Hebrews 2:14–15	Romans 7
John 14:6	Matthew 23:4
Genesis 3:5–6	Leviticus 17:11
Psalm 14:3	Romans 8:32
Psalm 51:16	1 Corinthians 11:24–30

John 19:30–36	Luke 23:34
Galatians 5:1	John 6:53–66
John 12:23	Romans 6:1–7
Luke 10	2 Corinthians 12:7–9
Acts 4:12	James 4:6
Romans 10:13	Proverbs 3:34
Acts 3:6	Exodus 4:10–11
Acts 3:16	Numbers 20:6–12
Genesis 4:10	

CHAPTER 10

The Battering Ram

Some stories in the Bible are lengthy and thrilling, while others are brief and bizarre. If you've been praying for a breakthrough, you'll want to take notes from a surprising place. Although the chapter tells an incredibly short story, the prophetic encounter teaches us about a massive key we need in order to see our *breakthrough* emerge.

This story comes from 2 Kings, Chapter 13. It begins with an important man who has a dire prayer request. The two main characters are King Jehoash and the prophet Elisha, and the scene is set in the middle of a bloody war. Elisha, now an old man, has come to the end of his life when King Jehoash pays a visit. At the time, Israel was in the throes of battle with the Arameans when the King comes to Elisha's bedside crying out, "My father, my father, the chariots and horsemen of Israel!" The nation's great strategist is grieved by the outlook of the war. His nation is in absolute jeopardy, so when he cries about the chariots and horsemen of Israel, he is lamenting over a military that's doomed along with his nation. To make matters more humiliating and shocking, this is the last man on earth anyone expected to approach

God's prophet! This is the very same king who had previously killed the prophet Zechariah, so for the man to come to Elisha's bedside for a word from the Lord shows he is desperate for help. This is an intense and undignified moment; the king has hit rock bottom! Despite years of dishonoring God, he *knows* he can't rescue Israel and he needs help from Heaven.

After Jehoash bares his heart and pours all his grief out on the table, Elisha, this interesting old man, tells him to grab a bow and arrows, *and in total seriousness*, he tells the king to strike the ground. *Can you imagine?* The two of them are alone together in the dying man's room, and Elisha wants him to perform this melodramatic act without further instruction on its reason or purpose. This is all in the midst of a national crisis! The king is waiting for a serious word from God on how to not get slaughtered, and he's instead told to perform an exercise. If the hot-headed man had killed a prophet in the past, he may have certainly wanted to chop Elisha right then and there for being told by an old kook to smack some sticks on the ground when he asked for militant instruction! It's a bizarre and telling moment as the king remembers why he's come so far from his palace to this humbler home, and sets his focus on performing the task. The king humbles himself, and he strikes the ground three times.

As I read this, I nearly clapped for the king! I was honestly impressed by his compliance. If it were me, I would have felt bashful. I would have felt silly and half-heartedly carried out the awkward act that seemed pointless, humiliating, and beneath me! I was almost amazed by the king until the next verse, where we see Elisha isn't impressed, he isn't one bit satisfied! Here's what verse 19 says, "The man of God was angry with him and said, "*You should have struck the ground five or six times;* then you would have defeated Aram and completely destroyed it. But now you will defeat it only three times."

The disappointed prophet left me speechless! What a rebuke, and a strange one at that. As I read those verses over again, I became fixated on how strange the story was, and I could not wrap my mind around why Elisha would reprimand a man for failing a test he thought he surely passed! He struck the ground three times, so what made his obedience insufficient? What did the prophet see that was amiss to me? Was Jehoash bashful, was he embarrassed, was he holding back because it felt like a silly thing for a king to do? I started to re-read the details and wondered what went wrong. The short story was packed into just six verses so I asked God to expound. I asked, "Lord, there is a mystery here, what is it?"

He said to me, *"Your victory is in proportion to the display of your desperation."*

I was shocked by the reply. I repeated the words back to God as I turned them over in my mind, *"Your victory is in proportion to the display of your desperation."*

I was amazed by that statement. I realized that even though it looked to me like King Jehoash had complied, Elisha's response showed me that the king was only doing the bare minimum because of pride. Pride and humility are a lot like oil and water, they repel each other, and oil (pride) is always going to dominate. If we hold onto pride, we end up *repelling* humility. The two are aggressively at odds with one another. In the case of the king, he wanted to be humble but when the oil and water tossed around in his heart, the oil came out on top. What is in our hearts determines how the Lord helps us, because He resists the proud and shows favor to the humble (Proverbs 3:34). God desires to help us, but pride will prevent us from appealing to God in humility.

Humility makes a difference to God. Speaking of another king, the Bible actually mentions who was the most corrupt of all. Ahab is declared the evilest king, a man who sold himself to wickedness (1 Kings 21:25). When Ahab learned of the Lord's judgment over his life for his sins, he humbled himself through fasting and mourning. When the Lord saw Ahab's fasting, He was willing to help even the most wicked of kings because of the man's *humility*. God spoke to the prophet Elijah, saying, "See how Ahab has humbled himself before Me? Because he has humbled himself before Me, I will not bring the calamity in his days. In the days of his son I will bring the calamity on his house." (1 Kings 21:29 [NKJV]). There is something important to catch here about becoming humble in order to display our desperation for God's intervention.

> **Your victory is in proportion to the display of your desperation.**

If God will show mercy on evil people who humble themselves, how much more will God do for those who are humble and pure hearted? Through these stories, I learned that our victory is given to us in *proportion* to our *display of desperation*. Humility makes big appeals in God's Kingdom. We don't want to hold anything back from showing God how much we need Him! Jehoash failed this test, but I can point to another man who broke through. And this is where we come to the topic of fasting as a prayer approach.

DANIEL: A DESPERATE DISPLAY

Who is the man who put his desperation on display? That would be Daniel. Here was a man who received dreams and visions, many of which their interpretations could have gotten him killed had God not been on his side. At one point in his life, Daniel was fasting and praying for three weeks because of a certain vision he had received pertaining to a great war. He had no clue what the vision meant, but it was clearly to impact the entire nation of Israel, so instead of forgetting about the vision or making up his own interpretation to avoid his homework, he pressed in with great focus. Daniel decided to use fasting and prayer. Daniel, Chapter 10, says he was in *mourning*; that's the level of desperation he displayed. He was grieved to understand the mysteries of Heaven, and he positioned himself to appeal for revelation and understanding. At the end of the three weeks, Daniel found himself standing before a heavenly messenger. (Daniel doesn't mention an angel this time, he actually describes the messenger as a "man". There are varying opinions as to whether this heavenly man was the angel Gabriel or Jesus Christ. For simplicity, I will refer to the heavenly man as a "messenger".)

I appreciate that in documenting his own story, Daniel withheld no dignity! He openly and vulnerably accounts how desperate he was to receive the revelation, documenting how he contended for the breakthrough with extended fasting, prayer, and mourning. Despite his determination to communicate with Heaven, when he finally receives a reply from a magnificent supernatural man, Daniel becomes so overwhelmed that he passes out before ever hearing the message! So of course, the messenger wakes him up. Imagine that the same heavenly being who terrified you into passing out is the same one who startles you awake again. Talk about a waking nightmare! Seeing the poor man trembling on the ground, the messenger had to strengthen and encourage Daniel so he could stand and receive the revelation he had been contending for! (God literally lends us Heaven's strength and encouragement in order to receive Heaven's communication.)

After strengthening Daniel, the messenger says, "Don't be afraid, Daniel. Since the first day you began to pray for understanding and to humble yourself before your God, your request has been heard in Heaven. I have come in answer to your prayer." (Daniel 10:12 [NLT]). The messenger says something very important that shows us the dispatch time for Heaven's response. Daniel had been fasting, praying, and mourning for twenty-one days, *humbling himself before God*. Daniel had been contending for three whole weeks, but it wasn't until twenty-one days later that he finally got a reply. The messenger says something that shows us how Heaven's response time works in partnership with our efforts, but also in confrontation with opposition. The messenger essentially explains to Daniel, "I know I'm here three weeks later, but we actually received your call on day one!"

When it comes to our prayers, do you think there is a lag time in Heaven between the call center and dispatch team? When you cry out to Heaven, does dispatch send out a team on day one, or do they mull it over and take it up the chain and decide to dispatch three weeks later? We find our answer in reviewing what the messenger told Daniel had happened between day one and day twenty-one of his fasting. The messenger says, "But for twenty-one days…". (There it is, Heaven dispatched help on day one.) "But for twenty-one days the spirit prince of the kingdom of Persia blocked my way. Then Michael, one of the archangels, came to help me, and I left him there with the spirit prince of the kingdom of Persia. Now I am here to explain what will happen to your people in the future, for this vision concerns a time yet to come." (Daniel 10:13–14 [NLT]). This account tells us so much about Heaven's timely response to our prayers. Although Daniel didn't hear back for three weeks, Heaven sent help on the first day he set out to fast and pray. We know this because the messenger told Daniel, "Now I am here, but I was blocked by the spirit prince of the kingdom of Persia for twenty-one days!" Heaven replies to our prayers and sends help, but there are times when our breakthrough comes into confrontation with strongholds and hold ups.

Not only do angels encounter demonic strongholds in the heavenlies, but we encounter the same strongholds on our end. It's like we're attacking the same tower from different sides. The angels come from their direction, and we come from ours. The messenger got through because Daniel refused to give up, although he felt a block in the spirit he kept praying until that block moved and he got his reply. Daniel didn't give up praying. How many of us give up on our request before dispatch ever reaches us? Don't hang up the phone. Help is on the way.

THE HOLD UP

Ephesians 6:12 says, "For our battle is not against flesh and blood, but against the rulers, against the authorities, against the powers of this dark world, and against the spiritual forces of evil in the heavenly realms." That is displayed in this story. Daniel had no idea what was happening between day one and twenty-one, he was not privy to the forces of resistance. Nevertheless, Daniel knew one thing; He still didn't have his answer! This should be a lesson to us all. Just because it's quiet on our end doesn't mean Heaven isn't making big moves on their end. We don't know what kind of opposition our miracles and messengers are coming into, so we need to keep praying. Although Daniel didn't hear back for three weeks, he never let up on his spiritual action plan. He fasted and prayed without relenting.

Finally, one of God's mighty archangels arrives to deal with this hold up. As Michael intercepts the demonic spirit prince, Daniel's messenger is able to break away and reach him, showing up to the bank of the Tigris river with a dazzling body and a voice like the sound of a multitude. With this voice, the messenger explains the meaning of Daniel's vision.

Through this story, we witness spiritual defense, offense, interception, and partnership. This tells us there are demonic forces that are opposing heavenly forces—sometimes even delaying our breakthroughs. When it comes to the supernatural, there are very real strongholds at play!

When Ephesians 6 tells us that our battle is against spiritual forces, it instructs us to arm ourselves accordingly! We are told we are at war with spiritual forces, but the Bible doesn't leave us hanging, we are given spiritual armor for spiritual battle! Therefore, it can be concluded that what stands between the prayer and breakthrough *is the spiritual battle!* There is a force of resistance at work.

> *We are given spiritual armor for spiritual battle.*

The messenger who came to Daniel explained he had been "blocked". A comparison of the various translations corroborates a scene of great opposition in which the spirit prince of Persia was "resisting", "opposing", "blocking", "withstanding", and "fighting" the messenger. The enemy resists us, stubbornly! Even Jesus taught on this when He addressed stubborn demons. When His disciples asked about certain demons not being cast out on the first try, Jesus told them that certain ones only come out by *prayer and fasting*. In Mark, Chapter 9, Jesus' disciples are dealing with a deaf and mute spirit that they can't drive out. Jesus explained, "This kind can come forth by nothing, but by prayer and fasting." (Mark 9:29 [KJV]). When Jesus says, "this kind", what kind of demon does He mean? Is He speaking specifically of spirits that manifest in deafness and refuse to listen, or of impure spirits, or of spirits that have bound the person since childhood? All of these traits are mentioned. Whatever the case, Jesus is teaching about *stubborn demons*.

Our Lord told us, plainly and point-blank, that certain battles require further measures and levels of persistence. In fact, He said certain demons come out by *nothing* but prayer and fasting. (Some of you are one fast away from your victory!) It should not surprise us, then, when certain strongholds in our lives don't seem to budge. This need not discourage us, because a stubborn stronghold tattles on itself—it actually tells us everything we need to know in order to overcome it. Jesus already told us that to overthrow stubborn demons, we must activate prayer and fasting. I call this weapon the *battering ram*.

Do you know what a battering ram is? You've probably seen it in a movie when an army takes a giant log or tree and batters it like a ram's horn against a medieval fortress. In other words, the tool is used to breach massive fortifications. 2 Corinthians 10:4 tells us that we have been given *weapons* of *warfare* that are not carnal, but mighty through God to the *tearing down* of *strongholds*. Isn't that the definition of a battering ram? Fasting is one of those weapons of warfare that can tear down a stronghold like a powerful *battering ram*. When you don't see a stronghold go down on the first blow, persistent fasting and prayer causes that stronghold to splinter and weaken until you punch through! Finally, that stronghold crumbles under its own weight and what was once a tower is no more than a pile of dust.

> *To overthrow stubborn demons, we must activate prayer and fasting.*

Do you see that Daniel didn't just say a prayer on day one or day two and then quit? No, he applied pressure! He was so desperate for revelation that he prayed for twenty-one days. He didn't just say a prayer once a day and hope that was enough. He used fasting to position himself into mourning. He was *grieved to receive!* That's why Michael came to assist the messenger who was being blocked. The archangel turned his attention to someone who was putting their desperation on full display. *Fasting is a head turner!* You must know, we are in a battle, and our persistence matters. Persistent people don't pray once and call it a day. Fasting is like going on a hunger strike if I can put it that way.

HUNGER STRIKE

Consider the hunger strikes you've seen in the news. When people really want to see change, they go on a hunger strike and what this does is it grabs the attention of the person who can make that change. It's an alert to the one who has the power to help them. When I am fasting and I get the munchies, and I'm looking at the cabinet and my stomach is growling, here's what I say, "Lord, I am on a hunger strike. I admit, I am really hungry, but I'm not hungry for anything more than I am hungry for a breakthrough. Lord, I am desperate, but I admit I am most desperate for a breakthrough." That's my petition.

Once while fasting I wrote down, "I'm *starving* for a breakthrough, I'm *hungry* for Heaven, I'm *fatigued* but sustained by the spirit, I'm *desperate* for a response!" Fasting is like a hunger strike that positions you to say nothing, not even food, is more important than receiving Heaven's help. In fact, Paul says our weapons of warfare are not carnal, but they are mighty in God. Fasting is the least carnal thing you can do. Fasting decreases how much you are operating in your carnality because as you deny yourself fuel, your human strength rapidly weakens. This is the point of fasting—you come to depend on God's strength and not your own. It's interesting to note who usually delivers God's most important messages, and that is the angel Gabriel, who Daniel encountered in earlier visions. In Hebrew, Gabriel's name means, "Strength of God" or "God is my strength". When God sends you help, He sends you *His* strength. If you need God's help and strength, try fasting, it's a voluntary act that denies you of your own strength and appeals to God for His strength. How? It causes your flesh to go to the wayside so your spirit can step up to the frontline and deal with things. This is a weapon that is not carnal, but mighty in God!

NEW TESTAMENT FASTING

While I launched into the topic of fasting with Old Testament references, it was actually in the New Testament where I realized the power and value of fasting. Something shifted in me when I studied the life of Jesus. I began to pay close attention to anything Jesus ever said or did.

If Jesus valued the power of prayer and developed a dedicated prayer life, then I better have a dedicated prayer life. Jesus taught about fasting on several occasions. In Matthew 6:16 He rebukes the hypocrites who make a spectacle out of their fasting and instructs us to prepare ourselves and dress ourselves as usual, so that no one but God would know we are fasting. In this teaching, He doesn't make a suggestion to the people, saying, "*If* you fast, do it this way." Actually, He says, "*When* you fast, do it this way." In saying this, He characterizes praying people as fasting people. In 1 Corinthians 7:5 Jesus gives instructions to married couples about how to devote themselves to times of fasting and prayer under agreed terms so they do not deprive one another of intimacy. Not only did Jesus teach on fasting, but He fasted as well, most notably before the onset of His public ministry. Jesus was led by the Holy Spirit into the wilderness where He fasted in solitude for 40 days and nights. He used fasting to prepare Himself for public ministry and all that it would cost Him. During those 40 days, He denied Himself the desires of His flesh in order to seek the Lord's will.

When you deny your flesh its essential needs, you *subdue* your flesh. Your body needs food to survive. By withholding food, you are showing your flesh that nothing, not even your own self, is more important than what God wants. It's not easy to go inside your soul and subdue your mind, will, and emotions. Yet these are the areas that need to be starved, detoxed, weakened, crucified, taken captive, and surrendered. The body is only the vessel of the soul. *Your body never does anything without the command of your soul.* If you've had a bad day and your *emotions* want comfort food, and you *will* it so, and your *mind* says, "Eat it", then your body goes and gobbles down everything in your pantry. Fasting disrupts and re-orders the direction of cause and effect. Whatever the flesh does is downstream of what your soul has willed forth. Starving the flesh removes the vessel from the equation so you can make progress upstream. This work is done by your spirit. Matthew 26:41 tells us, "The spirit is willing but the flesh is weak". When your spirit subdues the flesh and cuts it off from taking orders from the soul, suddenly the vessel of your soul is out of the way and now you can deal directly with central command. Fasting puts the flesh aside so your spirit can step in and deal with the soul.

I believe Jesus' fasting and prayer played a crucial role in Him being able to surrender His will for God's will. Although Jesus was God in the flesh, He was still fully human just as much as He was fully God. This was by design. Christ had His own thoughts, will, and emotions that were naturally human. In Luke 22:42 we see Christ's humanity in full bloom when He asks the Father to remove the "cup of suffering".

In the Garden of Gethsemane, Jesus struggled for us. He wrestled His own will for our sake. Luke 22:44 says Jesus was in *anguish and agony*. Luke depicts His sweat to be like drops of blood. While this picture is usually overlooked as just a simile, Luke is a doctor so he's more likely drawing reference to Hematidrosis, a rare condition in which a person's sweat really does contain blood. This occurs when a capillary blood vessel that feeds into the sweat glands ruptures, causing a person to exude blood in their face. *The cause of this condition is extreme physical or emotional stress.* This is the type of agony the doctor is describing Christ to have endured the night before He was crucified. Jesus was sick over the thought of crucifixion. According to Luke 22:44, this agony drove Jesus into more fervent and earnest prayer. We know what this prayer was, "Not my will but yours be done." (Luke 22:42)

Christ had His own desires; they didn't just disappear after fasting in the wilderness. Even in His last moments, He was found having to surrender His will. Our "God in the flesh" Messiah desired to live and not die, to be spared and not suffer. Even in His last moments, He was found having to surrender His will in anguish. I believe the 40 days of fasting before the onset of His public ministry was a time when Jesus had already made up His mind. He was going to subdue His flesh and surrender His will no matter the cost. If Christ needed prayer and fasting to surrender His will for God's will, how much more do we have need?

Galatians 5:17 says our flesh and spirit are at *war* with one another. If you don't arrest your flesh, your flesh and spirit will be at constant odds! This is not the way we want to live, so how do we get ahead of this? How do we crush the flesh and hand over the reins to our spirit? In writing to the Corinthians, Paul explained that he is running a race to win a prize. He says that instead of running aimlessly or fighting like a boxer who beats the air, he goes into strict training. Of this training, he says, "I strike a blow to my body and make it my slave." (1 Corinthians 9:27) That's how serious Paul was. He didn't cater to his flesh, in fact, he arrested his flesh and put it under the will of his spirit so he could win his prize! Fasting will help you do just that. Leviticus 23:27 says fasting *afflicts* the soul. It's for serious competitors only!

If you have faith for a breakthrough but your prayers don't seem to be making the cut, add in fasting! This is biblical. Paul said he fasted *often*. In his second letter to the Corinthians, Paul is talking about how much he has served and suffered. It is very clear, from stonings to shipwrecks, that Paul was frequently in need of a breakthrough. He was in constant need of Heaven's help, so he made a *routine of fasting* and *fasted often!* I might not identify with Paul's sufferings, but I know that I'm always in need of Heaven's help. I myself am finding that I go from needing one miracle to the next.

If you need routine breakthroughs, you might need to implement routine fasting. Routine fasting for routine breakthroughs. If you feel like you are constantly on the defensive instead of the offensive, try getting ahead with fasting. I used to be a spiritual push-over. Fasting took me from being in the trenches of the battlefield to the ramparts, because fasting is a weapon of warfare! What does fasting accomplish in the spirit? It would take a whole book to cover all the purposes and outcomes of fasting, so let's cover just a few.

> *If you need routine breakthroughs, you might need to implement routine fasting. Routine fasting for routine breakthroughs.*

OUTCOMES OF FASTING

We may use fasting for a multitude of reasons, and in hopes of different outcomes. There are private personal fasts as well as corporate fasts. Reasons we might fast are for repentance and setting ourselves right before the Lord, because we are in a battle and we need help, because we need strategy and answers, or because we are overcoming temptation. While it's a healthy practice to take a break from entertainment and social media, the biblical weapon is the fasting of food. You might find mental refreshment from other forms of fasting, and you might even find spiritual refreshment by replacing all that time of scrolling with scripture. However, it is through the biblical fasting of food by which you will see miracles, breakthroughs, and answered prayers.

There is a fast for everyone, even those with health complications. There is the total fasting of food and water which was done by Esther in a life-or-death situation. There is the fasting of food accompanied by water intake. There is also the Daniel fast where he eliminated "choice foods" and stuck to the basics. People might fast one meal a day for a week, or they might fast one day in full, or up to twenty-one days like Daniel, or forty days like Jesus. (Before you fast, it is critical you research how to safely sustain and exit the fast, such as how to re-introduce food to avoid complications, hospitalization, and in extreme cases, death. Use wisdom, do your research, and consult a doctor.) You will see people fast in different ways, and your own fasting routine may evolve from season to season.

What's critical for every fast, though, is fasting with a pure heart.

The entire theme of Isaiah 58 is how the *results* of your fast depend on your heart. The writer describes how the Israelites worked hard to fast, pray, and seek God for answers and help, but at the end of the day, nothing changed. Why? Because when you cry out through your fasting and proclaim that you are humbling yourself to God, but your heart is still ugly and sinful, your fasting means nothing. It's a cheap performance and empty appeal. You starved yourself for nothing, because you cannot say to God, "I am humbling myself, Lord. I love You and honor You, and I ask You to help me.", while you sin, mistreat others, and behave poorly. You cannot go on displeasing God and expect your fasting to do you any good! This is the theme of Isaiah 58. The Israelites asked God, "Why have we fasted, and you have not seen it? Why have we humbled ourselves, and you have not noticed?" To which

God replied, "You cannot fast as you do today and expect your voice to be heard on high." (Isaiah 58:3–4).

What does it mean, then, if we fast, pray, and humble ourselves correctly? *Our voice is heard on high!* This does not mean that God does not hear us in our sin. Our sin does not make Him deaf to our cry, our sin makes Him unresponsive to our cry. Consider a courtroom. When a case is *heard*, this means it moves forward in the hearings. The case is selected and pulled from a pile of cases that is stacked from floor to ceiling. The judge takes that one case and separates it from the rest and *hears* it. That's the term. When a case is heard, it is taken from among all the rest, and it is helped.

God always hears us but fasting compels Him to review our case. It's an act of faith that says, "Most High Judge, please hear my case!" It's your appeal to the courtroom of Heaven, and Isaiah 58:4 indicates that when you humble yourself and fast rightly that your voice *is heard on high*. In one translation, Isaiah 58 is titled "Fasting that Pleases God". In another translation it's titled, "True Fasting". It would benefit you greatly to read Isaiah 58 to learn about what true fasting looks like. When you fast in a way that pleases God, you can expect things to *break forth suddenly, to appear quickly, and to receive God's help, protection, and His personal reply*. Have you been praying for a miracle to break forth and quickly appear? Isaiah 58:8–9 links fasting to these results:

> *Then your light will break forth like the dawn,*
>
> *and your healing will quickly appear;*
>
> *then your righteousness will go before you,*
>
> *and the glory of the Lord will be your rear guard.*

Then you will call, and the Lord will answer;

you will cry for help, and he will say: Here am I…

We see the Holy Spirit drawing Jesus into the wilderness to fast, and while there are certain occasions for which you will experience the Lord's leading, it's typically our call to initiate the fast. It's your request that you are contending for, so it's up to you to initiate. Remember, you are sending an alert to the one who has the power to help you, and you're not hanging up the phone until you receive help. But you can't wait around for a suggestion from Heaven to fast. You've read here about the outcomes of a fast that pleases God, and you can use fasting to turn to God for help all the same. Daniel 9:3 says that Daniel *turned to the Lord* and *pleaded with Him in prayer and fasting*. When we fast, God takes notice that we are initiating a request for help. Fasting causes us to turn to God and wait on Him. When God sees you aren't seeking help from anywhere else, it's a wonderful opportunity for God to do what only God can do. One of the most memorable examples of a fast for urgent help came from the command of a king in trouble. In 2 Chronicles, King Jehoshaphat was surrounded by three oncoming armies, and instead of panicking and fretting over impending doom, the Bible says that when the king became alarmed, he resolved to inquire of the Lord. Instead of overworking himself on the military plan, he switched his response and battle tactic to seek the Lord. He did this by calling for a nationwide fast. Not only did the king fast, but he called a corporate fast for the entire nation; He commanded that his people participate with him (2 Chronicles 20:3–4).

King Jehoshaphat was faced with a national crisis and an oncoming army, and though he was extremely alarmed, he resolved to look to God. To think, I get knots in my stomach over the day to day of my unpredictable life! Yet when this man was under military pressure, he resolved to stop *everything* and turn to God. When our circumstances are alarming to us, and when we would prefer to quit, or fall on our sword, or grab the alcohol and drink it all away, fasting will resolve us to stop everything and go to God for help. Fasting forgoes any other vice, comfort, or crutch that our flesh might look to. Fasting arrests our flesh from freaking out, giving up, or trying to take control. It causes our flesh to back up so our spirit can come to the forefront and appeal to Heaven. This is what fasting does for us.

In Joel 2:12 God calls His people to return to Him through fasting. He couples the command by saying, "Return to me with all your heart". There is something about fasting when it's paired with prayer that causes our whole heart to return to God. In Psalm 69:10 David says that he humbled his soul with fasting. When we give up food and our stomach starts to growl forty-five minutes into the fast, we start to realize how weak and needy we are. Fasting humbles us. It causes us to recognize our own needs and desperations and yet we lay it all down as a petition to Heaven to provide for us.

Ahab was described as the most evil king in the entire Bible, and yet because he turned to God with fasting and prayer, God gave mercy even to the most evil king! That's saying a lot. Fasting can humble the most evil and lost of us all because when we admit our own weakness and cry out for God, we are returning to Him with our whole heart. This is so important. When we are finally humble, we can plead with God in prayer and petition, and seek help from the Lord. *If you need help, which we all do, these are keys for you!* Fasting humbles you, it positions you to look to God and plead with Him, but what happens in the spiritual realm? This is where things get exciting!

USE FASTING AS A BATTERING RAM

The idea of the battering ram came into my life during one of my fasts. I committed to a certain fasting routine while I was in prayer about something, and I repeated it day after day because I felt like my fasting was breaking through. Suddenly, one day I started to hear something in my spirit. I heard it over and over again every time I fasted. I heard the words, *"battering ram"*.

Not knowing much about what I was hearing, I looked it up and learned that a battering ram is a powerful piece of equipment. It's a weapon of warfare that was invented by the Assyrians. Modern battering rams are handheld because they need only to bust through the depth of a two-inch door, but back when the Assyrians designed this thing it was of colossal size. They roped this massive log on a huge frame so that it swung back and forth like a pendulum. Battering rams were known to be effective weapons of warfare because they had the ability to breach massive fortresses. Realize that this ingenious weapon was merely a swinging log. It was the *tactic* that was the key. If that log could be persistent in applying pressure and deliver repetitive strikes, then dents would turn into cracks and cracks would turn into holes. *Battering rams are designed to tear down strongholds!*

Fasting has the same impact. As you can see from the scriptures above, fasting was often done in times of warfare and distress because it is a mighty weapon of warfare. When I heard the words "battering ram" in my spirit while I was fasting and found out it was a weapon of warfare to tear down strongholds, I recalled what I knew of Isaiah 58:4. Fasting that pleases God causes a breaking forth and quick appearance! When Daniel's reply was held up by a demonic stronghold, his fasting caused a breaking forth and quick appearance. If you feel like you've been waiting for an answered prayer for ages, add in fasting! It brings out the *battering ram*.

SIEGE WARFARE

The battering ram is a specific type of weapon for something called siege warfare. Beth Van Schaack is an Ambassador-at-Large for the Office of Global Criminal Justice. On February 4th, 2016, she wrote an article for Just Security, titled, *Siege Warfare and the Starvation of Civilians as a Weapon of War and War Crime*. In this article, Beth explains that siege warfare "involves surrounding a garrison or a populated area with the goal of driving out the enemy forces by *deteriorating their defenses* and cutting them off from reinforcements and vital supplies."[19] Because a siege is a long-term tactic, it is typical for the invading forces to set up some type of military blockade, fortress, or *stronghold* to serve as their base of operations. In other words, if the enemy can't outright overtake you, he will set up a stronghold outside your gates so he can afflict you over time.

While this type of warfare sounds intense, it is actually a sign of weakness from the invading forces. Siege comes from the Latin word which means to sit. When an enemy doesn't have the power to overtake a territory immediately, they resort to sitting on it *over time*, using strongholds and constant pressure to deteriorate their rival's defenses. Schaack remarks that while a siege is less intense and usually less deadly

---

19   Van Schaack, Beth, *Siege Warfare and the Starvation of Civilians as a Weapon of War and War Crime* (February 4, 2016), https://www.justsecurity.org/29157/siege-warfare-starvation-civilians-war-crime.

than an open battle, it is a costly and time-consuming method of warfare—for both parties.

As I learned about siege warfare, I realized how often the enemy uses this tactic, and what that means for us. Ever since Satan was cast out of Heaven, he's been setting up strongholds on the earth and in the heavenlies and working to lay siege to God's Kingdom and all that belongs to Him. Remember, siege warfare and the use of strongholds is an invader's tactic to conquer a kingdom and seize the throne room, which is exactly what Satan is trying to do! But we know how this story ends. The book of Revelation makes it clear that Satan will not overtake our kingdom, and the enemy will be defeated. Just because we know how the battle ends, doesn't mean we don't have warfare today. The enemy is advancing on believers by setting up strongholds that are costly, time-consuming, and deteriorating to our lives. Satan may have power to set up strongholds, but guess who has the power to tear them down? We do! And if we have power to tear down strongholds, you better believe God gave us weapons to do just that!

Realize this. The enemy is sitting on you for a reason. You have something inside of you that he cannot overpower, and that is Christ in you, with the power of His name, His blood, His victory, and His authority. When the enemy sits, it's a sign for you to *hit*. Siege warfare is all that the kingdom of darkness has on us. Since the enemy is not strong enough to overpower Christ in us, he can only sit on us by putting up strongholds and fortresses. A siege only lasts for as long as you allow. *So, are you gonna' let the enemy sit on you? Or are you gonna' roll out the battering ram and start making toothpicks out of strongholds?*

Fasting splinters strongholds. It applies constant pressure until a stronghold comes down. With every swing of that battering ram, the hit becomes stronger, and stronger, and stronger until it punches through! Those ancient walls were not all that strong. Sure, they looked big, but they were actually weak in tension and prone to cracking when impacted with force! Strongholds come down under constant pressure. Sometimes our breakthroughs are held back by strongholds, and some of those strongholds don't come down on the first blow—they take splintering. Fear not. You have a mighty weapon to do just that!

TACTICAL TRAINING

Drill In

Read: Isaiah 58:1–9

Reflect: Can you spot the benefits of fasting correctly and the consequences of fasting incorrectly? Underline or meditate on the following notes in this passage. When you fast correctly your voice is heard on high. When you fast in a way that pleases God, you can expect things to break forth suddenly and to appear quickly, and to receive God's help, protection, and His personal reply.

Read: 2 Chronicles 20:1–30

Reflect: When trouble is on the horizon, our first instinct is usually to rally the forces for action. Instead, this king's militant tactic was to stop everything and proclaim a nationwide fast. Meditate on the passage and be encouraged by God's response.

Read: Mark 9:14–29, Esther Ch. 3 and 4, Daniel Ch. 9 and 10, Matthew 6:16–18, Matthew 4:1–11, Leviticus 23:27, Psalm 69:10

Reflect: Jesus told us that certain demons can only be cast out by prayer and fasting. As you read through these passages, make note of other reasons people fasted. What was the outcome?

Drill Out

We are almost ready to complete our battle plan to tear down strongholds. First, let's run some drills with our battering ram. Joel 2:12 says that when we fast, our hearts return to God. Can you see how fasting is a way to bring you closer to Jesus?

Consider how you can fast this week. If you are new to fasting, you may want to consider a set of mini-fasts to train your body, mind, and spirit before attempting a longer fast. Once you've decided how you'll fast, begin to take your needs before God. Request an outcome and contend for a sudden breaking forth and quick appearance. Don't just reflect on your needs, though, but use fasting to come close to your sweet provider and deliverer. The Father.

Drill Down

    2 Kings 13   **Luke 22:42–44**

    1 Kings 21:25–29   **Galatians 5:17**

    1 Corinthians 7:5   **1 Corinthians 9:27**

CHAPTER 11

Prayer Tactics for Whoopin'

One of my greatest fears is rushing water. In my travels to Africa and Central America, I've encountered countless moments where I refused to wade into the dicey waters. I've had friends who were daring enough to swim in risky seas or cross through rushing rivers, and I flat out refused. Once, my friends held hands to human-link themselves across a raging river so they could continue our hike up a mountain. I parked my butt on a rock and waited until they finished the hike and turned back around. I refused to step foot in that raging river. One time, though, I couldn't back out from the activity, all because of some children!

In 2013, I went to Costa Rica with twenty other members from my church. About half of the team was comprised of college students, and the other half was made up of families with children, some as young as seven years old. It was the most children I had ever traveled with. The kids impressed me as they ventured through the flights, layovers, and airports to get down to Costa Rica, and then we entered the foreign country. This took over eight hours, but they handled it all with a great attitude. Immediately afterwards, we loaded up on a bus for a six-hour drive to the remote jungle. Tired from the journey so far, the kiddos dozed off on the long bus ride. Daytime passed, the sun set, and we drove into the night. For the children, though, they awoke to a time lapse and got dumped in the jungle. This is when panic broke across their faces.

When the kids awoke from their naps, they walked out into the pitch-black darkness of a secluded wilderness. As their eyes adjusted to the midnight obscurity, they beheld a vast and muddy jungle that was anything but familiar to them. To add more of a dramatic flair, lightning dashed across the endless sky and exposed, just for a moment, the mysterious jungle that surrounded the cabin. The flash of light went as quickly as it came, and the tree line disappeared into the night! Alas, it dawned on the children that they were in the middle of nowhere and surrounded by the unforgiving wilderness, one they could not even see. We unloaded the bus, showed the kids their cots, and started to unwind for bed. To my surprise, all hell broke loose as the children spiraled into sheer hysteria. The darkness, exhaustion, the lack of air conditioning, the jungle noises, the lizards, spiders, and mosquitoes—it all caused an uproar among the children!

The tables turned, though, and I was humbled by these youngsters on the last day of the trip. The team leaders worked out an activity for the group and we all got dropped off at one of Costa Rica's famous spots for whitewater rafting. Now I was the panicked one. The guides began organizing the team to fill out consent forms, break off into groups, and get fitted for gear. I stayed at the end of the line, fully expecting that one of the children would back out and I could volunteer to stay behind and babysit. (So selfless of me, I know!) To my dismay, I was disappointed when they all ran to the front of the line and were the first ones to sign up. They were excited, eager, and jumping up in synchronized squealing and squawking! My friend looked at me with a head tilt and said, "If the children are all doing it, you can't back out."

The only thing I remember from those next two hours is the break we took on shore halfway through the expedition. (I probably kissed the land.) I gorged myself on the tropical watermelon and pineapple just in case it was my last meal ever. I literally remember nothing else. I blacked out the experience *while* I was in it. The only thing I have to bring color back to my memory of that day are the photos of me wincing and hiding behind my oar. Darn, those brave children!

As we close out your time in this book and charge you to take your stand in the place of prayer, I'm hearing the tune of a children's song sing loud and clear. Perhaps you know it. The song is called, "I'm In The Lord's Army". I think this song will encourage you, and if you can look up the music video, you might just get goosebumps as you watch children in camp uniforms lift their little legs to march with confidence, swinging around their toy weapons. Because this is the heart of a child—brazen and fearless! Nothing exudes more confidence than a child who knows they want to do something, and by golly, they're gonna' do it! Christ said the Kingdom of God belongs to those who are childlike (Matthew 19:14). *Timidity and disbelief are the fruit of an adult who has aged without childlikeness in the Lord.* If you need a fellow soldier to give you a daring pep talk and to give you the boost you need, accept the charge from children!

I dare you to look up this music video by the Cedarmont Kids[20], to get up off your couch, lift your legs, swing your arms, and sing along (as of this writing it has 7,439,852 views)! If you need courage in the Lord, you may need to deal with the timidity and disbelief of the adult mind. *Become childlike.* Sing along, "I'm in the Lord's army, yes sir!"

"I'm In The Lord's Army"

Sung to tune of Old Gray Mare,
Author Unknown[21]

I may never march in the infantry

Ride in the cavalry

Shoot the artillery

I may never shoot for the enemy

But I'm in the Lord's army!

I'm in the Lord's army!

Yes Sir!

After Paul teaches us about spiritual warfare and tells us to use our armor and weapons, he concludes this charge by telling us to pray in the Spirit always, with all kinds of prayers and requests, and on all

---

20   Cedarmont Kids, *I'm In The Lord's Army* (October 17, 2013), https://youtu.be/nJoB5XCQ5gs.
21   Derocher, Matthew, story behind the song *In the Lord's Army?* (August 03, 2021), https://theformer.faith/en/post/in-the-lord-s-army.

occasions (Ephesians 6:18). Paul is telling us that there are so many reasons to pray, that we should be so inclined to pray on all occasions, and that these different reasons to pray are going to cause us to pray in different ways. As you read through the Bible and watch people pray, you will find them praying for different things and in manners appropriate to the cause. You will find times to pray with worship and praise, petition and intercession, supplication, thanksgiving, and even spiritual warfare. I would go on to corporate prayer, the prayer of faith, the prayer of tongues, the prayer of the Holy Spirit, etc. These are just a few examples of different types of prayer, it need not be over complicated. Let me put it in layman's terms. Prayer is you communing and communicating with God, and God communing and communicating with you.

As you communicate with God, He charges you to deal with things. If you've been living bound, He will charge you according to His Word to be free in Christ! If you've been hindered by setbacks, He might just tell you, "Speak to that mountain and tell it to move!" He will charge you to defend yourself according to His word and the authority He's already passed on to you! Whatever you need and whatever you need to address, you can do so by tailoring your prayer approaches as the Lord leads you. This is the versatility that Paul is charging you with, "And pray in the Spirit on all occasions with all kinds of prayers and requests." (Ephesians 6:18).

> *Prayer is you communing and communicating with God, and God communing and communicating with you. As you communicate with God, He charges you to deal with things.*

For the purposes of tearing down the strongholds in your life, we are going to conclude with some tools to use when the "occasion" for prayer is spiritual warfare. This is going to be a rapid fire training as we move quickly through the tools and tactics, because it's time to get you off the page and into prayer. No more dilly-dallying. Here are some tools and tactics you can use to begin tearing down strongholds biblically, wisely, and confidently. *Yes sir!*

PUT ON THE ARMOR OF GOD

The Bible is clear that in order to stand firm against the Devil's schemes, you need the armor of God. Ephesians 6:11 says you must put on the armor in order *to take your stand against the Devil's schemes*. Ephesians 6:13 says you will stand firm even after the battle. This is the protection of God's armor, it keeps you sturdy in God's mighty power. As you begin to take your stand, the very first thing you will want to do is to make sure you're wearing your armor. You don't want to show up naked and uncovered. While David denied Saul's offer for the king's wonderful armor, he did not go to battle uncovered. David was covered and armed with the *name* of the Lord. If our battle is a spiritual one, then natural armor will do us no good. God has given you fitting armor for the occasion.

Right as I was finishing the manuscript for this book, I experienced an overwhelming amount of spiritual warfare. The warfare was so real, I was afraid the Devil was going to kill me. While I was in prayer, I felt peace come over my head. I asked the Holy Spirit what was happening, and I had a vision of the Lord tightening the helmet of salvation around my head. Then He strapped the breastplate of righteousness on me. He buckled the belt of truth around my waste, and He fitted my feet with the shoes of peace. Then He secured the shield of faith to my arm and put the sword of the Spirit in my hand. I looked at the sword and saw scriptures engraved all around it, beginning with Ephesians 6:18 (pray in the Spirit). This is God's armor for the believer. Each of these pieces carry indisputable truths and protection that will help you stand your ground against the Devil's schemes.

> *Finally, be strong in the Lord and in his mighty power. Put on the full armor of God, so that you can take your stand against the devil's schemes. For our struggle is not against flesh and blood, but against the rulers, against the authorities, against the powers of this dark world and against the spiritual forces of evil in the heavenly realms. Therefore put on the full armor of God, so that when the day of evil comes, you may be able to stand your ground, and after you have done everything, to stand. Stand firm then, with the belt of truth buckled around your waist, with the breastplate of righteousness in place, and with your feet fitted with the readiness that comes from the gospel of peace. In addition to all this, take up the shield*

of faith, with which you can extinguish all the flaming arrows of the evil one. Take the helmet of salvation and the sword of the Spirit, which is the word of God. (Ephesians 6:10–17)

BE STRENGTHENED IN THE LORD

Do you feel tired before you even start? I know the feeling! If you are reading this book, it is likely that you've been dealing with a stronghold for a long time, just like I did. By the time I was ready to take my stand, I was so tired I felt like a leaf blowing in the wind. I wondered how quickly the enemy would blow me over. This is a self-centered mindset, though. The Word of God tells us we need God's strength and not our own. The Lord wants to refresh and revive you, but don't believe the lie that you need to feel strong before you deal with your strongholds. You just need God's strength. Psalm 18 is a pretty gnarly chapter about how God hears us and fights for us. Psalm 18:1–3 says,

> *I love you, Lord, my strength*
>
> *The Lord is my rock, my fortress and my deliverer;*
>
> *my God is my rock, in whom I take refuge,*
>
> *my shield and the horn of my salvation, my stronghold.*
>
> *I called to the Lord, who is worthy of praise,*
>
> *and I have been saved from my enemies.*

The Lord is our strength, and He rescues us. Nehemiah 4:14 says, "After I looked things over, I stood up and said to the nobles, the officials and the rest of the people, 'Don't be afraid of them. Remember the Lord, who is great and awesome, and fight for your families, your sons and your daughters, your wives and your homes.'" As you deal with the spirit of heaviness, start by remembering how great and awesome our God is! Do not be afraid of how silly you look, how long this takes, how many times you have to try or shift the tactic, or how many times you have to start over. Don't be afraid. I charge you in the name of Jesus to *fight* for yourself and your bloodline. Remember how great our God is and you'll do just that!

Exodus 15:3 says, "The Lord is a warrior; the Lord is his name." Psalm 57:3 says, "He sends from heaven and saves me, rebuking those who hotly pursue me— God sends forth his love and his faithfulness." He is a mighty warrior who scatters our enemies! More than that, He is our refuge. While He is the one who does the heavy lifting, He still empowers you with His strength.

Zechariah 4:6 says mighty things are done by God's spirit, "'Not by might nor by power, but by my Spirit,' says the Lord Almighty." Philippians 4:13 says you can do all things through Christ who gives you strength! Psalm 18:39 says, "You armed me with strength for battle; you humbled my adversaries before me." Psalm 18 depicts a God who trains us for battle. With His strength we can advance against any troop, scale walls, stand on heights, and bend bows of bronze! Psalm 18:35 says, "You make your saving help my shield, and your right hand sustains me; your help has made me great."

It's God's strength we need. His help strengthens us and makes us great. I submit to you it's time to be great in God! 1 Samuel 30:6 says that David *strengthened himself* in the Lord. This was an independent and voluntary action, Daniel initiated the inner strengthening! He did not wait on his emotions to catch up to a good day before he strengthened himself in the Lord. 1 John 3:20 actually says God is greater than our feelings. We fight with God's strength, not our feelings, so you can be strengthened in the Lord on your good days and bad. Psalm 138:3 says, "You made me bold with strength in my soul" (NASB). If you feel tired, heavy, and weak, fear not, use scripture to strengthen yourself in the Lord. His power is perfected in our weakness (2 Corinthians 12:9), so your weakness is a great place to begin!

KNOW WHERE YOU SIT

If you've been a pushover and punching bag to the enemy, you need to remind yourself that you've been called to sit and reign with Christ. Ephesians 2:6 says, "God raised us up with Christ and seated us with him in the heavenly realms in Christ Jesus". *This is our seating assignment; we are seated with Christ.* 2 Timothy 2:12 says if we endure, we will reign with Him! We have been given a high position of rulership. Revelation 5:10 tells us we have been made kings and priests to our God, and we are charged to reign on the earth. There is absolutely no reason we should be taking any abuse from the enemy! We have been commanded to cast out devils and to partner with Christ in His mission to destroy the works of the Devil. We do this by knowing our identity, our authority, our seating assignment, our job description, and not taking any funny business from the enemy. The Devil also has a seating assignment, so go ahead and show him to his seat. Romans 16:20 tells us God will crush Satan under our feet, so put him in his place!

AGREE WITH GOD'S PLANS AND PURPOSES

If you're like me, you have no more time to waste. It's time to get free! The fast-pass to freedom is to agree with God's plans and purposes. So many people are stuck in bondage because they've come into agreement with it. They've agreed with bitterness, depression, heaviness, and sin. When you agree with your bondage, you forfeit agreement with God's Word. When you forfeit agreement with God's Word, you choose bondage over freedom. I learned a lot about coming into agreement with God's Word while I was in counseling for trauma and forgiveness. I wrestled, and wrestled, and wrestled with anger and bitterness. I was hindered for so many years because I kept waiting for this "feeling" to arise that would signal I was ready to forgive and let go. Finally, in my mentorship group with Jennifer Eivaz, she pointed out that if you're waiting for a good feeling to let things go, well, that day may never come. Jennifer told the group that we have to sow in faith. I began to sow my words even though my heart was not in it. I would begin to speak forgiveness in faith, because I knew it was more important to agree with God's Word than my feelings.

> *The fast-pass to freedom is to agree with God's plans and purposes.*

After sowing my words into forgiveness by faith, I eventually felt the forgiveness actually take root in my heart. I did the same thing with the torment that was happening. I sowed my words, time, prayers, tactics, focus, and attitude into believing I would be set free. I did this by faith and in agreement with God's Word. After six years of daily torment, one day became the last day, and I was suddenly free! After decades of watching pornography, you may not have faith that you can beat it. After spending so long with anxiety, depression, and PTSD, you may not have faith that you can defeat it. I want you to apply two principles:

1. You have to come into agreement with God's Word.
2. You have to sow in faith, not feelings.

AGREE WITH GOD'S WORD!

Christ has destroyed the works of the Devil, so we are no longer partners to sin!

> *The one who does what is sinful is of the devil, because the devil has been sinning from the beginning. The reason the Son of God appeared was to destroy the devil's work. (1 John 3:8)*

Christ sets free the captives and oppressed!

> *The Spirit of the Lord is on me, because he has anointed me to proclaim good news to the poor. He has sent me to proclaim freedom for the prisoners and recovery of sight for the blind, to set the oppressed free… (Luke 4:18)*

Christ sets you free—truly free!

> *So if the Son sets you free, you will be free indeed. (John 8:36)*

STAY UNDER THE COVERING

Psalm 91 speaks of the benefits we have when we remain under God's covering. He becomes our refuge and fortress, He rescues and protects us, but there is a specific location where you must place yourself—under the shelter and dwelling of the Most High. What the psalmist is saying is that *God Himself* is the shelter. He's the covering; He Himself is the refuge and fortress. When you make God your dwelling place, this means that wherever you go and whatever you do, He is your covering, literally not figuratively. Psalm 91:1–2 says, "Whoever dwells in the shelter of the Most High will rest in the shadow of the Almighty. I will say of the Lord, 'He is my refuge and my fortress, my God, in whom I trust.'" Psalm 91:4 says, "He will cover you with his feathers, and under his wings you will find refuge; his faithfulness will be your shield and rampart."

When we make God our covering, we are covered by fierce love and protection. As you begin to tear down the strongholds in your life and confront demonic assignments, you might need to change your address. Where has "home" been for you? Have you camped out in your own will, wisdom, and strength? Make your permanent address in "The Most High".

> *If you say, "The Lord is my refuge,"*
>
> *and you make the Most High your dwelling,*
>
> *no harm will overtake you,*
>
> *no disaster will come near your tent.*
>
> *For he will command his angels concerning you*

to guard you in all your ways;

they will lift you up in their hands,

so that you will not strike your foot against a stone.

You will tread on the lion and the cobra;

you will trample the great lion and the serpent.

"Because he loves me," says the Lord, "I will rescue him;

I will protect him, for he acknowledges my name.

He will call on me, and I will answer him;

I will be with him in trouble,

I will deliver him and honor him.

With long life I will satisfy him

and show him my salvation." (Psalm 91:9–16)

STAY UNDER THE HEEDING AND LEADING

The Holy Spirit will tell you what to do, when to do it, and where to go. Having the Holy Spirit's leading is extremely important, even life preserving. I have two friends who travel to a certain Islamic nation several times a year to witness, minister, and evangelize in the name of Jesus, which is totally illegal in that place. For discretionary purposes, let's call this country Agrabah. One friend was quietly wrestling with the concern of being jailed during his next trip to Agrabah. In fact, he was hearing an inner voice telling him he would be jailed. This friend needed to know if this voice was the Holy Spirit telling him not to go, or if the enemy was trying to intimidate him. If this was an intimidating voice from the enemy, then he would not complete his assignment for the Lord and souls would not be saved. But if this was the voice of the Holy Spirit trying to protect him from being locked up, then he better not take a chance. He prayed a simple prayer for God to clarify. This person wanted a pure answer from God, so he did not tell anyone else what was going on so he could limit the number of voices influencing a decision that could result in imprisonment, or worse. Not knowing anything about the matter, the Holy Spirit spoke to his ministry partner that same day and told him to tell his friend, "God says you will not be jailed in Agrabah." The Holy Spirit gave affirmation, and this person knew he could go to Agrabah with God's protection and favor and bind the voice of intimidation from interfering.

I've experienced similar heedings and leadings by the Holy Spirit that served to protect me. I was told about a car accident beforehand. God didn't tell me, "Stay off the roads for a few weeks". That was not the word for me. The word was, "Trust me". Another time the Lord showed me that a person in close proximity to my nonprofit had a bullying spirit that was about to explode on me. Over the next few months, God showed me steps to take to protect myself, which came in handy when this person ended up erupting out of absolutely nowhere. On another occasion, I was invited to minister with a team in Uganda. About two months before the trip, I received a startling dream. The dream revealed that our host would betray us. After waking up to a racing heart and pain in my body from the way this person attacked me in the dream, I half expected God to tell me not to go. But that was not the purpose of the dream. The purpose of the dream was to open our eyes so we could go, minister, restore order, and invite the pastor in sin to repent. This trip ended up taking a bad turn very quickly, and everything shook out just as the dream foretold. In this instance, the Holy Spirit gave both his *heeding* and *leading*.

A heed either comes as a red light or yellow light. A red light instructs you to stop and go no further, while a yellow light instructs you to proceed but with great caution that will preserve you. You do not want to confuse the two.

Paul was led in the same way. He had every intention to enter into Asia, but the Holy Spirit kept preventing him. Instead of going to Asia, the Holy Spirit instructed Paul to go to Jerusalem, where he ended up being arrested. Despite everyone's prophetic insight and heeding for him not to go, Paul knew he was meant to go based on the Holy Spirit's leading. (Sometimes you have a heed and you *still* have the lead.) We don't know why the Holy Spirit prevented him from entering Asia. On the other hand, we do know why the Holy Spirit led Paul to Jerusalem (Acts 23:11). When it comes to enemy territory, you have to be sure about the Holy Spirit's heeding and leading. Paul's friends pleaded with him not to go to Jerusalem. In fact, they gave him a prophetic word that he would be arrested. They cried and begged him not to go, then they had an emotional farewell because everyone knew it would be the last time they would see one another. Paul had to be sure about the Holy Spirit's leading, because while everyone else in his life tried to prevent him from going, he felt called and he had to follow God.

We know how the story ends. Paul's imprisonment was a win for the gospel. He was eventually transferred to Rome for trial, where he was able to witness to the gentile capitol of the world. The move of God took off all the more despite him being a prisoner! This is why the Holy Spirit's leading is so critical. He will heed you and lead you. Imprisonment can either serve to advance you or hinder you, so when the Holy Spirit speaks on the matter, you do not want to get the red lights and yellow lights confused. If Esther didn't have the correct leading to approach the king, she would have been hanged. If Ananias didn't have the correct leading to go to Saul, the famous persecutor, his house call could have resulted in a stoning to the death.

I tell you these stories to remind you to follow the heeding and leading of the Holy Spirit. Maybe you've heard about an awesome man or woman of God who confronted a principality or territorial spirit. Just because they had the assignment does not mean you do too. Stay in your lane, become mature, use wisdom, and wait for the leading. One night I woke up to a demonic spirit screaming at me. This encounter came after spending multiple weeks in prayer. I had been praying to see in the spirit because I had felt some type of resistance against me, and I could not put my finger on it. So, for weeks and weeks, I prayed for God to reveal to me the spirits on assignment in my life. I expected the Holy Spirit would reveal this to me by the gift of "discerning of spirits", but I definitely did not expect to encounter the thing. To my surprise, I awoke to an accusatory spirit screaming, "Pervert!" at my front door (literally).

What I've learned over the years is that a spirit's behavior reflects its assignment. This was the spirit of perversion, and it binds people through false accusations about their nature. Imagine growing up with parents who scream at you, "You're stupid!". What you believe shows through your behaviors. If you believe you are stupid, you will lose motivation to prove yourself in school and look for other ways to make a way in life—perhaps even through illegal or self-degrading means. However, if you know you are intelligent and that your parents are hateful liars, then you will apply your efforts in proving them wrong. Accusing someone's character and identity can have a dramatic effect on a person's life depending on what the person believes about themself. When I heard this spirit of perversion yelling accusations at my front door, I realized why so many people are stuck in perversion. It's because the enemy has accused people of being perverts by nature. For many, he is holding their sins and temptations over their head, saying, "You'll never overcome this because you are a pervert, it's in your DNA."

When someone believes they are something by nature, they will succumb to it because they believe it's innate to them—that it *is* them. People go back to pornography because they have no hope they can overcome their "nature". You have to know your true nature, so you won't believe the "accuser of the brethren" over your Father! 2 Peter 1:4 says we are partakers of *divine nature.* Your nature is freedom, authority, holiness, and righteousness in Christ Jesus! So how do you defeat an accusatory spirit? By knowing who you are in Christ and standing on His Word for your life. (This is good news for somebody!) You defeat a false accusation with the Truth!

Another behavior from this spirit of perversion was its door-to-door patrol. This spirit looks for open doors. By the grace of God, my door was shut. This encounter made a lot of sense as I processed it, because I have a testimony of my own where I had to fight for a life of purity, and I founded a ministry to fight against child sex trafficking. This ministry helps teenagers who have experienced child trafficking or exploitation to also live a life of healing, hope, and purity in Christ. Of course, the enemy would love nothing more than to stop all of this, so it should come as no surprise that the spirit of perversion would check on me and see if there is an open door to come in and destroy God's work. This was a territorial spirit, patrolling my neighborhood and working to raise up perverts, pedophiles, and sex addicts to keep sex trafficking alive in my state.

This felt like a very personal house call, not only to me but to the ministry. With this information, one might assume that I was supposed to confront this spirit. If I had not prayed about the matter, I might have entered into a direct spiritual assault on this spirit. But that is not the reason why God revealed it to me. In fact, the way I was to fight this spirit would be by living a clean life, calling other young people to purity, and by raising up my ministry. I didn't have to do anything in confrontation with that spirit, because I was already doing what I needed to do. I was defeating it by raising up a ministry to take back the territory! When I woke up, I prayed and asked God what I should do, if anything at all. One of the first things I heard was to keep shut doors *shut*, so I could maintain my authority over the assignment. If I did not ask Him what I should do, I would have perceived the encounter as a call to confront this territorial spirit. That may have resulted in me stepping outside of God's covering, and when you move out of your lane, you might get sideswiped by something you were never called to confront. Then, the Lord is going to have to rescue you and heal you from a battle He never sent you into. As you begin to confront the strongholds in your life, it is important to stay under the Holy Spirit's heeding and leading.

1 Corinthians 2:13 and Luke 12:12 tell us the Holy Spirit gives us the right words for spiritual matters and confrontations. As you begin to decree, declare, bind, loose, confront, cast down, rebuke, break curses, and pray in the spirit, ask the Holy Spirit to give you the right words. Isaiah 30:21 says you will hear a voice telling you which way to go; *wait on that voice!* Romans 8:26 says we don't even know how to pray for ourselves. Allow the Holy Spirit to intercede for you and give you the grace and instruction you need for your particular battle.

REPENT AND RENOUNCE

Earlier in the book we talked about how critical it is to clear out your house. When you begin the extermination process, you want to see it all the way through and not leave anything behind that could spring up with a new infestation. The actions of repenting and renouncing will help you to take those necessary steps. When John the Baptist prepared the way for Jesus, his message was, "Repent!"

Repentance involves an entire change in direction in which you turn away from your sins. You can feel sorry your whole life without ever actually repenting, this is otherwise known as shame. Repentance is not just feeling and saying sorry. It involves making a complete 180-degree U-turn in your life and fleeing from the direction of sin. In Genesis 4 we read about a conversation between God and Cain. The Lord told Cain that sin desired to have him, but he had to rule over it. The key, God said, was to do the right thing instead of the wrong thing. Simple, huh? This was before the law existed, and yet there was a right and wrong way. The Lord was adamant about helping Cain when he was plotting an evil deed, of which he unfortunately went through with. It really is the Lord's kindness that leads us to repentance (Romans 2:4).

> *You can feel sorry your whole life without ever actually repenting, this is otherwise known as shame.*

Paul tells us what happens when we repent, "Repent, then, and turn to God, so that your sins may be wiped out, that times of refreshing may come from the Lord." (Acts 3:19). When your sins are wiped out, you become blameless and perfect in the Lord, and the accuser of the brethren has nothing on you. The record is wiped clean! Repenting is critical for turning to God, but it's also a life saver when it comes to uprooting the footholds in your life that the enemy used to hold onto!

Sometimes repenting makes all the difference, and other times, you need to pair it with the act of renouncing. Proverbs 28:13 says, "Whoever conceals their sins does not prosper, but the one who confesses and renounces them finds mercy." I believe renouncing is the throwing off of sin that Hebrews 12:1 speaks of. When we repent, we turn. And when we renounce, we throw off. Renouncing helps to detach ourselves from what used to entangle us, it *severs the tie*. 2 Timothy 2:19 (WNT) says, "Let everyone who names the Name of the Lord renounce all wickedness." Renouncing something in the name of Jesus severs you from ties to wickedness, and it has the ability to break demonic partnerships, agreements, and covenants.

> *When we repent, we turn. And when we renounce, we throw off.*

When pastor and author Jennifer Eivaz came to Christ, she was tormented by evil spirits that were linked to the Satanic ritual abuse she experienced as a child. Even the deliverance ministers failed to detach her from these evil spirits. Finally, one day when the spirits came to torment her, she stood her ground and said, "I'm not going to serve you. I serve Jesus." With that, the spirits left and never harassed her again. You can take a straightforward approach and use the word "renounce", or like Jennifer, you can be empowered by the Holy Spirit to find another way to renounce spirits and throw them out of your life. Either way, rebellious spirits won't leave without an eviction notice and determined homeowner. So, open your mouth and say, "Time is up. Get out and don't come back!"

Some of you have tried to become free in the past and are discouraged by stubborn or returning spirits who have an attachment to you. I want to encourage you that the Father will back your renouncements. Have you ever realized how Satan mimics God? Just as God has a church, so does Satan. While Christians have words of knowledge, wisdom, and prophecy through the Holy Spirit, the occult uses demonic power to tap into fortune telling, which is knowledge from demonic sources. Where Christians speak in tongues, the occult has demonic tongues. These are just a few examples, although there are many more. Satan is a copycat, and he lures people in with counterfeits to the move of God.

In the same manner, Satan has mimicked the covenant as well. Why would he copy the covenant? The Word of God tells us we are the *bride* of Christ. We also know that when we receive Christ, we become *sealed* with the Holy Spirit. God's covenant seals us with Him, so of course the enemy would try to seal us to himself instead. Satanic worship involves covenant ceremonies, rituals, and marriages that dedicate and seal people to Satan.

I love the protective nature of a father and husband portrayed in Numbers 30. In the Old Testament if a young girl made the mistake of swearing to a vow she should not have agreed to, her father or husband had the power to annul her of the vow, and the Lord would absolve her. If that is the power of an earthly father and husband, imagine the authority of your Heavenly defense! God is your Father and Christ is your husband—and they can override your previous vows, covenants, contracts, decisions, and alliances! Sometimes we make foolish or harmful vows that can ruin our lives, but Christ can free us. He does more than divorce us from the vow, He annuls it. An annulment destroys the legal contract so that it becomes erased from record, as if it never existed. To renounce wickedness in the name of Jesus will annul any harmful covenant you've knowingly or unknowingly made with the enemy. When you renounce the Devil and ask your Father to back you up in the annulment, He overrides the contract the enemy has on you. When you repent of sins and renounce wickedness, stand on the Word that your loving Father and Heavenly Bridegroom have freed you and sealed you to them.

DECREE AND DECLARE

As you pray you will need to speak with authority and truth. You have probably heard people say, "In the name of Jesus I decree" or "I declare". You've probably also heard the two used in tandem, "I decree and declare". Consider their applications in a worldly sense. When a decree is made, it is an official order made by a legal authority. To declare, though, means "to make known" or "to set forth an accounting". One issues an order while the other issues a public declaration and claim.

When a person travels abroad they have to pass through customs and declare what they are carrying. After the customs agent clears you, you move on to the "baggage claim" and you claim what you just declared. When I am praying, I make declarations to declare truth in my life according to scripture, and I go home with what I've claimed. For example, I will say, "I declare that I am not anxious, because in everything I pray and give thanks to God. I tell God my requests and the peace of God, which surpasses all understanding, guards my heart and mind in Christ Jesus." By saying this, I am declaring Philippians 4:6–7 over my life. When you pray and make a declaration, you don't just declare something, you claim it. According to scripture, I can possess peace in Christ instead of anxiety, so I claim God's Word by making a declaration.

To make a decree is to issue an order. In Matthew 6:10 Jesus teaches us to pray for God's Kingdom to come and for His will to be done on earth as it is in Heaven. When we see God's truth and will stated in scripture, we can't be sitting ducks. We need to play our part as God's agents on earth and pray for His will to be fulfilled. There are times in prayer that we should ask God by requests (Matthew 7:7–11, Philippians 4:6–7) but many times we are begging for things that God has given us authority over. When you see God's truth, will, and promises in scripture, you can use scripture to decree God's will to be fulfilled on earth. When there is sickness, decree healing (Mark 16:18). When there is chaos, decree peace (Mark 4:39, John 14:27). When there is lack, decree provision and abundance (Psalm 34:10, Matthew 6:31–32, 2 Corinthians 9:8).

In some cases, you might decree and declare in the same statement. I do this often when I feel in limbo to my victory. I declare the truth and decree an order in tandem because although I believe God's Word, I am still working toward the victory. For example, when I had panic attacks, I said, "I decree and declare that by the stripes of Jesus I am healed of trauma and PTSD. I cast out every spirit of fear and death and I decree and declare I am free by the blood of Jesus!" This prayer helped me greatly, because although I believed God's Word and claimed it over my life for freedom and healing, I was still without the victory. I declared the truth and claimed it for myself. I also decreed an order that carried legal authority. I always tie my decrees and declarations to scripture because neither my mind, nor any argument, nor any devil can dispute scripture. When you decree scripture, you can enforce it all the way to victory. It is an insurmountable weapon.

BIND AND LOOSE

I've heard preachers teach differently regarding binding and loosing, so let's clear the air on the controversial topic. One opinion is that you should bind the activity of demons and loose the activities of Heaven. In this vein, a person might say, "I bind the spirit of fear from prospering in my life any further, and I now loose the spirit of power, love, and a sound mind!" This school of thought teaches that whatever you bind in regard to the enemy, there is a countermeasure to release from Heaven. The principle is that as you cast out the presence and torment of the enemy, you become filled with the presence and blessings of God.

There are people who believe that binding and loosing in this manner is wrong. These teachers and preachers (and YouTube ranters) propose the opposite. This school of thought proposes you should bind yourself to the blessings of Heaven and loose yourself from the torment of Hell. For example, according to this group, if you say, "I bind the spirit of infirmity and loose healing to me in the name of Jesus", they believe that you've just tightened the enemy's grip on you by binding him to you, and you've disbanded the efforts of Heaven by sending them away from you. This group believes that you MUST say it in reverse, "I loose myself from the spirit of lust and bind myself to purity and righteousness."

To summarize, one school of thought proposes you should bind the activities of the enemy and loose the activities of Heaven, while the other proposes the opposite. If you think about it, it's a matter of semantics, perception, and intent. I propose you can bind whatever you want, and loose whatever you want, in whatever words you choose to use—as long as your intent is clear in what the words mean to you. The key is to listen to the Holy Spirit, to use your authority in the name of Jesus, and to use your words with wisdom and purpose. Jesus and the disciples delivered people in a variety of manners. In one case, Jesus was dealing with a spirit of infirmity that had tormented a woman for eighteen years. He did not rebuke or bind the spirit, He said, "Woman, you are loosed from your infirmity!" (Luke 13:12). After He loosed her from the spirit, then He laid hands on her and she was healed. In this case, Jesus chose to loose her. The disciples, though, casted out devils by rebuking them and commanding them to leave.

Matthew 16:19 authorizes us to decide what we bind and loose, using a key word—*Whatever*. Whatsoever we bind on earth will be bound in Heaven. And whatsoever we loose on earth will be loosed in Heaven. You have been authorized to decide those factors by the leading of the Holy Spirit, so do not let someone else cause you to overthink or complicate the practice of binding and loosing or casting out devils. *Children* are casting out devils, former Muslims and atheists who are but a day old in Christ are casting out devils. I know of former Muslims right now who became saved in Christ and that same day they went to the streets to heal the sick and cast out devils. They were not concerned about learning how to tailor their words because they were empowered by the Holy Spirit and authority of Christ. I look back on my journal and I can point out a few prayers that I would edit today but guess what—those prayers worked and I'm free! You don't need to string together a perfect set of words for your authority to work—that's the trash they teach witches, to speak incantations in perfectly practiced and pronounced Latin.

Don't overthink or complicate the matter. The authority of Christ in you is what speaks volumes. Let the Holy Spirit mature your speech as you walk it out. Luke 10:20 says the spirits are subject to *you*. You can decide what to bind and loose, and the boundary line is "whatever". If you want to bind the spirit of addiction from operating any further and loose the fruit of self-control, go ahead. If you want to bind yourself to truth and mercy (Proverbs 3:3) and loose yourself from the spirit of confusion and pride, do that. Be free and take care of business.

DEAL WITH THE DOORMAN AND STRONGMAN

Jesus tells a story in Matthew 12:43–45 about a demonic spirit who is forced to leave his house. After some time roaming about, the spirit returns to his former house to check on his previous real estate. Is the door closed, are they renting to new tenants, has the house been sold to Christ? The spirit returns and finds the house unoccupied, swept clean, and put in order. This spirit likes what he sees—his old house looks cozy and inviting, no one else has claimed ownership yet, and he wishes to overtake it once again. The problem, though, is this defiled spirit has already been kicked out once before, so he is not strong enough to occupy the space all on his own. This time, the spirit goes to his friends and tells them he has a wonderful house. Jesus clarified this house to be a man. In Matthew 12:43 Jesus says the evil spirit left a *man*, and in the next verse, that spirit calls the man his *house*. So, the demon returns to his old house and brings with him seven spirits who are "more wicked than itself".

When you are writing out your prayers and identifying which strongholds need to come down, you will want to identify the spirits behind that stronghold. Who came in and set up shop? That's who you're evicting! In your worksheet, you will need to list out every single evil spirit that's been working in your life. Use the "Hit List" at the end of this book and be thorough. I think The Message translation puts it just about as real as it can get. Matthew 12:45 (MSG) says evil spirits come to *"whoop it up"* in your life, and in your house. According to Jesus, *you* are the house. Some spirits will have a stronger grip and assignment in your life, but do not leave out the minor ones as well. If anything has been "whooping it up" in your house, it's time to whoop its defiled butt to the curb. Once you've listed out all of the spirits that have been "whooping it up" in your life, you are going to single out two of them: *the first and the strongest.* Pay attention! This is a big key!

Demonic spirits work together to "whoop it up" in your life. In another instance, Jesus was dealing with a demon who called himself "Legion" because there were many spirits in one person. Demons come in packs. When one comes in, it wants to throw a house party, so the first spirit opens the door to numerous others. Isaiah Saldivar is one of my most trusted sources for teachings surrounding deliverance. I like how he puts it, "You don't get to decide what comes in."[22] If you have an open door of pornography, you don't get to decide whether or not a spirit of suicide gets to come in. The first spirit to come in holds the door open for numerous others to come in with it. In the story from

---

[22] Saldivar, Isaiah, paraphrased from *Revival Lifestyle Podcast* messages and used with permission. You can listen to them at https://revivallifestyle.libsyn.com/. You can learn more about Isaiah Saldivar at https://www.isaiahsaldivar.com.

Mattew 12, notice how the *original* spirit brought in *seven stronger spirits*.

While there are numerous spirits that you'll be binding and casting out of your life, the *first* spirit and the *strongest* spirit are the two that you want to give special attention to. Sometimes these two spirits are one in the same. For example, this was the case over my life. When I listed out every spirit "whooping it up" in my life, I circled the spirit of fear. This was the strongest spirit at work. It was the reason behind my PTSD, my choking, my breathing issues, my panic attacks, and my anxiety. All of these symptoms made me feel like I was dying, like I was living a nightmare, and like my world was falling apart. The spirit of fear was tormenting me. When I traced this spirit all the way back to where it entered, I realized it was the very first spirit to whoop it up in my life. When I lost my father at a young age, fear entered my life—fear of loss, death, abandonment, and the unknown.

For me, the first spirit in my life was also the strongest spirit. I circled this spirit on my hit list and gave it special attention. Other times, though, the first spirit merely serves as the "doorman"—the one who opens the door to let in stronger spirits, as is the case in Matthew 12. Whatever the case, the two menaces that are calling the shots are very likely the first spirit and the strongest. Whether they are two separate spirits or one in the same, identify these suckers and aim the bullseye right at them. *When they're gone, the weaker spirits will be easier to cast out because the doorman and the strongman have been evicted.*

Remember, there is absolutely no reason you should be afraid of demons. The only time I was ever afraid of a demon was because I watched a horror movie and dashed through my bedroom in the dark before that imaginary slimeball could get me! One day it dawned on me, I was more afraid of the demons I saw on my Netflix screen than

I ever was of the real ones I had so closely encountered. This is the handiwork of Satan trying to intimidate us. If he can puff up his minions through gory cinematic effects that terrify Christians, and send them jumping under the covers at the flip of the light switch, then we will have an upside down view of our authority over the kingdom of darkness—all because of good acting, a chilling soundtrack, and stage makeup!

Unfortunately, though, we have many Christians who are not only afraid of evil spirits, but they are also afraid of deliverance ministry and teaching coming into their church. How satisfied the enemy must be! No wonder so many people are in bondage. We've got Christians afraid of deliverance in the House of God! My favorite is when I hear a Christian talk about deliverance by saying, "That's demonic!". Well, no duh! The manifestation you are seeing is verifiably demonic. But the deliverance is by the power of God.

Dealing with demons is one of the primary charges we have been given by Christ Himself. He told us to cast out devils. But the Western Christian church has steered far away from this practice, and even separates themselves from those who try to restore this ministry and teaching back to the church. Casting out devils is supposed to be a wonderful part of ministry. Do you not recall the times the disciples ran back to Jesus in excitement, all because they had casted out devils? The result is freedom! This is an exciting work of God. Deliverance is part of the Gospel of Jesus Christ and brings God glory. This is the very point Jesus made to the Pharisees when they attributed casting out devils as the work of Satan. They had the same thought, "That's demonic!" (Matthew 12:25). Jesus explained to them that when demons are cast out, this is a sign that God's Kingdom is among us. Deliverance is God's power at work, and we are assigned to the job! We are the ones to be feared. I want to share with you the tactic that tied everything together for me and gave me a straight line to victory. When you hunker down and do this, it will be game over.

TACTICAL TRAINING

Drill In

Read: Romans 12:2

Reflect: The fast-pass to freedom is to agree with God's plans and purposes for your life. How do you do that? By coming into agreement with His Word. Are there any scriptures that are standing out as key weapons for your particular battle? Use scripture to renew your mind and agree with God's plans, purposes, and Word for your life!

Read: Acts 2:38, 2 Timothy 2:19

Reflect: When we repent, we turn from sin. And when we renounce, we throw off any attachment or bondage to wickedness. Is there anything you feel you need to repent of or renounce so that you can walk in full redemption and freedom?

Read: Matthew 12:43–45

Reflect: In reading this story that Jesus told, what stands out to you? Consider how Jesus talks about the one spirit who opens the door, and the seven spirits who are stronger. Ask the Holy Spirit to teach you how to bind and cast out these menaces.

Drill Out

By now, you should have your targets identified and your scriptural ammo loaded (sections one and two of *The Shotgun Sniper Worksheet*). Let's complete your biblical strategy to tear down strongholds! It's time to fire God's Word at those targets and take them out once and for all! You'll do this through prayer. Turn to the worksheet and take a look at *section three*. This is where you will write a scripture-packed warfare prayer.

Before you get to work, though, take a look at the *Example Prayer* in the Appendix. Read through and take note how scripture is used to run both offense and defense. I used scripture as ammo to take down the enemy, and I also used scripture to fortify my faith and defend myself against the enemy's lies.

Use the prayer tactics from this chapter and follow the format from the "Example Prayer" to prepare a scripturally guided prayer to take down the enemy and destroy strongholds. Remember, ask the Holy Spirit to lead you, and stay under the Father's covering.

Drill Down

This chapter was filled with important scriptures, so the list is pretty long. The next chapter doesn't have so many, so feel free to spread them out, if that's the way the Spirit leads you.

Matthew 19:14	Genesis 4
Psalm 138:3	Acts 3:19
Nehemiah 4:14	Proverbs 28:13
Exodus 15:3	Hebrews 12:1
1 Samuel 30:6	Numbers 30
Ephesians 2:6	Philippians 4:6–7
2 Timothy 2:12	Matthew 6:10
Revelation 5:10	Matthew 6:31–32
Acts 23:11	Matthew 7:7–11
2 Peter 1:4	Mark 4:39
1 Corinthians 2:13	Psalm 34:10
Luke 12:12	2 Corinthians 9:8
Isaiah 30:21	Matthew 12:25
Romans 8:26	

CHAPTER 12

The Power of a Plan

Have you heard this saying before? *"If you want something you've never had, you must be willing to do something you've never done."* This powerful quote is attributed to Thomas Jefferson. If you keep doing the same things over and over again, you're going to get the same exact results that you have now. Are you satisfied with those results? Have they led to freedom, peace and life in abundance through Christ? If the answer is no, it's time to try a strategic and coordinated prayer approach.

I wasn't just a sitting duck all those years, I prayed many times to be free and I was always disappointed. I went through a lengthy inner healing process, I commanded strongholds to fall in the name of Jesus, I had powerful ministers lay hands on me, and when none of that worked, I prayed for the fire of God to do what I could not. In the end, nothing broke the strongholds that were crushing me, and I was becoming increasingly discouraged about my authority.

After that crazy mind-binding attack and the word of knowledge that showed me everything was linked together, I stopped all of my tactless swinging. If I didn't have a plan, if I didn't have a target and strategy, I was going to spend the rest of my life swinging in the dark at a piñata that just dodged me, all to hit me upside the head on its way back around! I wasn't going to do the blind dance anymore. This time when I went into prayer, I asked the Lord for the strategy to finish the thing. This is when God showed me the importance of having a *plan*. Yes, a plan.

When the Israelites crossed over into the wilderness it took them several years just to become *organized*. They could not have completed the charge to clear out and occupy the Promised Land without being militantly organized. Here's the power of a plan. You write down the target, and you don't stop until you reach it. When you stick to a plan, it always results in victory because you don't stop until the job is done.

All those years when I prayed my prayers, said my decrees, and broke my ties to trauma, they fell to the wayside because of my wishy-washiness. I lacked a plan, so every time a new wave came over me, it would overwhelm me. A new wave would crush me, drown me, terrify me, and wash me back up to shore, beaten and disheveled. When I came up for air, I spiraled into timidity. I thought, "Why didn't that work? Why didn't I destroy it? Why is this thing back? What is the open door? What did I do wrong? Why didn't my faith crush this? Why doesn't my authority work?". Every time I would take a step forward, something else would show up and wipe me out back to square one of being intimidated and spiritually clueless.

This roller coaster type of scenario is classic to how abusers keep their victims in the relationship. Abusers give you just enough time to stand up and dust yourself off so you can have a few good days, and then they start the cycle all over again. Keeping a person on an emotional roller coaster of false highs continues to give you false hope that the abuse is over. The abuser will hurt you and run you into the ground until you stand up and defend yourself. Finally, when you can't take any more of their abuse and you get ready to end the relationship, they switch gears and say, "I love you.". The abuser doesn't want you to get the guts to leave. They don't want you to come to your senses. They don't want the fog to lift. Instead, they'll lift the abuse for a short time to confuse you. They begin to treat you well, they touch you tenderly, they speak to you kindly, buy you gifts, and take you on dates. You think, "Everything is better! It's all over! Everything has changed!" Believing that the abuse is a thing of the past, you stay. Just when the abuser has you convinced that everything is better, the abuse resumes all over again. This is how abusers use a roller coaster of highs and lows to confuse their victims.

This is what the enemy did to me, and this is how he kept me confused all those years. One week I'd be crushed, barely able to function or breathe or leave my house, and just before I would get the motivation to press into prayer for the strategy to break the thing, *it would lift*. I would have an amazing month without any issues, and I'd think, "It's gone!". Instead of standing up to the bully like I intended, I would sit down and kick up my feet, thinking the abuse was over. It wasn't until years later that I realized I had actually *never* gotten around to tactfully fighting this thing, not once! I truly never did. I said a prayer here and there, but never once did I attempt any real strategy against the enemy. Not once did I carry out a real assault. That's because every time I came close to being fed up and doing something about it… the torment would suddenly lift. This was how the enemy kept me on a trauma loop. The highs and lows caused me to be totally confused because when it appeared to be "gone", I thought I had overcome it. I was naive and overwhelmed, which allowed this to go on for far too long. Finally, the Lord revealed to me my problem was that I lacked a *plan*.

Do you know why the Israelites had so many issues with idolatry? They were on a loop of their own. When the Israelites began to seize the Promised Land, God commanded them to *clear* the land and leave "no living thing" behind (Deuteronomy 20:16–18). Unfortunately, they didn't finish the job. They allowed a few nations to stay in the land and this resulted in intermarrying. Intermarrying was the primary reason why Israel could not get rid of their idolatry problem. Their foreign spouses and neighbors influenced the Israelites with idol worship and pagan practices, and as hard as they tried, every time they cleansed the land of idolatry, it would spring up again.

Sticking to the plan is so important, because if you don't get the job done, whatever you leave behind will infest the land like weeds and bedbugs. You can't leave behind even one thing or it will multiply into an infestation. The Israelites thought they had conquered enough, so they kicked up their feet prematurely. When they conquered the big bad wolves in the land, they didn't see any problem with taking a few wives, although the instruction was to entirely clear the land. They lost sight of the plan and the few stragglers that remained were the very ones who kept them on a merry-go-round of strongholds for generations! In other words, *they kept going in circles on the same issue.* Why? Because they lost sight of the *plan* that was supposed to nip idolatry in the bud. Remember, if you give the Devil an inch, he will take a mile.

I realized that I had to clear the land and leave no survivors, or I would be stuck on this merry-go-round of the rest of my life. Finally, I went to the Lord and waited on Him for the strategy. What He spoke to me was the secret move for overcoming the Devil. In prayer, I heard, *"Wear him out!"* He was speaking of James 4:7, which tells us that the Devil flees when we *resist* him!

It's important that you realize what "resisting" is *not*. Resisting is not ignoring the Devil, and it is not avoiding eye contact. Here's how the Merriam-Webster Dictionary defines "Resist": "to *exert force* in *opposition*", "to *exert* oneself so as to counteract or *defeat*", and "to *withstand the force* or effect of". To clarify my point further, here are the synonyms and antonyms of resist:

Synonyms: buck, defy, fight, oppose, repel, withstand

Antonyms: bow (to), capitulate (to), give in (to), knuckle under (to), stoop (to), submit (to), succumb (to), surrender (to), yield (to)

As you can see, resisting the Devil requires a militant approach. Resisting is not hands off. It's sleeves up and earrings off. *You're gonna' throw some punches, baby.* Clobber the Devil with a left hook and right hook. Throw punches with the name and blood of Jesus! You have militant weapons that are designed to tear down, take captive, and make obedient (2 Corinthians 10:5). Your weapons can do all of this, but you have to stand your ground (Ephesians 6:14, "stand firm") and resist the enemy until he buckles. If you want the Devil to bow, capitulate, give in, knuckle under, stoop, submit, succumb, surrender, and yield… *then you better buck, defy, fight, oppose, repel, and withstand!* For this is resisting the Devil!

The greatest threat to your success is your short-sightedness, doubt, feelings, and wishy-washiness. There will be days when you don't feel like standing your ground. In fact, most days, you probably won't feel like fighting. I didn't have strength on my side, I had desperation. Most days I did not feel like praying. I just knew I was desperate and that was all I needed to see this through. Having a plan was my winning move.

It caused me to finally clear the land. I cleared out every last stronghold, and I left no survivors and no stronghold standing. This was the first time I had ever stood up to defend myself, to use my weapons, and to fight for the freedom that is promised unto me. I had no idea if it would work, I just knew what the Bible told me. Resist, and the Devil will flee! That was my approach, and my target was total freedom.

I learned a lesson from the Israelites quitting too early and I wanted to avoid making the same mistake, so I created a measuring stick (figuratively speaking) to make sure I didn't kick my feet up prematurely. This measuring stick didn't have centimeters and inches inscribed on it, it had two words, *"total freedom"*. I had been living my whole life in this notion that partial freedom was better than nothing. This is how the Devil keeps us from fulfilling our destinies. This is how he keeps us from having the mind of Christ. All those years, I thought partial freedom was good enough because what remained must have been the proverbial "thorn in my flesh" that made Christ's power all the more perfect in my weakness. Since I didn't know how to win, I used scripture as my crutch instead of my weapon. I pleaded the thorn and not the blood! But those days are now over.

In order to clear the land, I held up this measuring stick to assess my work. Every time I experienced one stronghold go down, I would pull out the tool and measure my results according to my target. I would examine the land and ask myself, "Have I reached total freedom?". If the answer was no, *then I did not let up!* The target was total freedom and nothing less! To that end, I woke up every morning and facilitated my plan in faith and militancy. In my journal, I wrote down every last target. Then I detailed out my tactics and weapons and backed them up with God's Word. Then I crafted a prayer that focused on tearing down every last stronghold. I laced in the name and blood of Jesus,

THE POWER OF A PLAN

I took communion with that prayer, and I made a plan for fasting. I loaded the "Shotgun Sniper" every morning and detonated it in the enemy's face. I told God, "I'm going to do this every day until every single stronghold breaks. Even if it takes the rest of my life."

It took me two weeks to break a six-year attack on my life. I was shocked and amazed. However long it takes for you, I charge you in the name of Jesus Christ to not stop until you have total freedom.

I urge you, friend, not to forgo the importance of forming your plan before you begin. It will prevent you from quitting prematurely, and it will be the key to your success. *Clear the land, leave no survivors, and make every last stronghold go boom!*

TACTICAL TRAINING

Drill In

The Plan:

Deuteronomy 20:16–18
Clear the land and leave no survivors.

Psalm 18:37–38
Don't stop until you conquer the enemy.

James 4:7
Resist the Devil. Wear him out!

Ephesians 6:13–14
Stand your ground.

The Results:

James 4:7
The enemy flees from you.

Psalm 18:37–38
The enemy can't get back up.

John 8:36, Galatians 5:1, 2 Corinthians 3:17
You have total freedom.

John 14:27, 2 Timothy 1:7, John 10:10
You have peace, a sound mind, and life in abundance.

Drill Out

When the enemy tries to keep you on the merry-go-round, having a plan will keep you steady and focused—paving a straight line to the victory! Let's turn now to section four of *The Shotgun Sniper Worksheet* and seek the Lord about two essential keys to the plan. Thoughtfully answer these two questions, "When will you pray?" and "How will you fast?"

Meditate on the scriptures above and ask the Lord to guide you on making a prayer plan. I activated my prayer strategy in full every morning for two weeks and finally, a six-year attack on my life was overthrown and I've been free since. It might take you longer or shorter, it might take you five minutes a day or one hour—the Lord will show you. The important thing is to not stop until you have total freedom. If you're not free, you're not done. Stick to the plan. Resist the Devil until he flees.

Drill Down

Ephesians 6:1

CHAPTER 13

Dealing with Return Visitors

When I got my freedom restored to me, it was like waking up from a bad dream. I could not believe what had happened to me, and I was so glad it was over. It was like a hypnotic fog had lifted. For six years, I felt like I was drowning, like I constantly had someone's hand pushing me under water. When my breath was restored to me, when the chains lifted off of me, when the torment was destroyed and the enemy put under my feet, *I realized I had forgotten what freedom felt like!* I remember driving down the road in total amazement. I felt free all the way from the valleys below to the sky far above. I felt freedom that stretched infinitely high, deep, wide, and far. I felt freedom in my mind, in my breath, in my soul, and in my spirit. For about a month's time I kept saying to myself, "This is freedom? It's so amazing…". Realizing the joy of freedom was a blissful experience, it was engraved into my heart with absolute wonder and gratitude.

After I began to tell my testimony, though, all of those wretched torments returned! It was as sinister as the Message translation describes it, when the evil spirit said, "I'll go back to my old haunt." (Matthew

12:45 [MSG]). I remember preaching about my testimony one night and as soon as my sermon ended, I went into the hallway and experienced a terrible panic attack. My throat closed up, I was choking again, and I felt like I was spiraling back into the same old. I quickly wondered if I was a hypocrite for teaching a sermon on freedom. *How could I be free if it was so easy for the enemy to just shove me back under again?* I quickly wondered if my freedom was all a ruse. *Had the enemy given me some time off to dash my hopes even further—all to blindside me with a stronger hand?* I wondered if my weapons of warfare and prayer tactics had any real power against the terrible torments! These thoughts came and went quickly, because when I got in my car, I adjusted the rearview mirror to look myself in the eyes, and I said ferociously, *"Do it again!"*

For the next few days, those panic attacks and torments tried to intimidate me and convince me I was not free. When I went back into prayer, I opened up the same journal I had been working from, and I spoke aloud, "If it worked once, it will work again!" With that, I activated my biblical tactics to tear down strongholds a second time. I used the same strategy until I had my freedom again! This time, it only took a few days.

What would have happened if I doubted my freedom in the first place? What would have happened if I just assumed my weapons of warfare couldn't do the deed? What would have happened if I got tired (and I was tired!) and called it quits? Those return visitors would have come in with a band of stronger friends and my final condition may have been worse off than my first (Matthew 12:45).

Have you ever dealt with an ex-boyfriend or girlfriend who won't buzz off? They come back periodically to see if they can weasel their way back into your life. They'll even come back to see if their stuff is still laying around—that would surely give them a claim to come inside! These spirits try to find a foothold to grab back onto or a door to enter through. This is why it's so critical to clear out the house. You've got to conduct a thorough extermination so that nothing remains.

When those spirits came back, I had a short moment of fear. I was afraid they were back because I wasn't strong enough the first time. But after tasting real peace, I was not about to give up my freedom. And I was not about to doubt my weapons of warfare, so I told those spirits to scram. They didn't know if I was serious, so I had to show them. They had been in my life for six years. They knew the old Cara, the one who was a pushover and punching bag, and they thought they could get back into the house. I told those spirits, "I am not your house anymore! And none of your stuff is here, I burned it all."

If you get your freedom and you experience any backlash, *stand your ground.* Ephesians 6:13–14 says that after you've done everything you can possibly do, you need to stand firm. When Jesus cast out the evil spirit from the little boy, He said, "I command you to come out of this child and never enter him again!" (Mark 9:25). If deliverance was final for a lifetime, why would Jesus need to tell a spirit to never return? Again, we cannot expect rebellious spirits to not rebel. Jesus taught on returning spirits, and He handled those spirits in His deliverances by *forbidding* them to return!

Evil spirits have predictable habits. While returning spirits are frustrating to deal with, we at least have foresight in how to arm ourselves accordingly. From time to time they might check in on their old stomping ground. But like the spirit that was surveying my front door, they can't come in if your doors are *shut*. The first step to protecting yourself from breaches is to shut all of your doors. Don't go back into sin. Don't go back to the footholds. Don't spare your favorite sweater from the bonfire. Shut the back doors, the side doors, and the trap doors. Don't you dare crack them open to check up on your old life—seal them shut and leave them. If your doors are shut and you feel pushback, then all you need to do is stand your ground. If your doors are shut, the only thing the enemy can do is try to use lies, intimidation, or temptation. *Resist him*, and he will flee.

The Message translation concludes the parable of the returning spirit by putting it this way, "That's what this generation is like: You may think you have cleaned out the junk from your lives and gotten ready for God, but you weren't hospitable to my kingdom message, and now all the devils are moving back in." (Matthew 12:45 [MSG]). Notice, the reason the evil spirit was able to reclaim his old home was because the man was not hospitable to the kingdom message. When we reject the Gospel, we can do all the spring cleaning we want, but we leave ourselves exposed because we've not given our house over to God. Although the evil spirit observed a clean house upon his return, he wasn't deterred by the cleanliness. Seeing an opportunity, he remarked, *"It's unoccupied!"*, because the homeowner hadn't brought in a new tenant.

We must occupy ourselves with the Gospel of Jesus Christ and be filled with the Holy Spirit. Colossians 1:6 says the gospel bears fruit by changing lives. If you receive the kingdom message, your life *changes*. When your life changes, a devil will not peep into your windows and say, "That's a clean and empty house". No, it will see a clean house that is filled with the Holy Spirit. If your doors are shut and you've occupied your home with the Holy Spirit, don't let surveyors worry you about your freedom. Defend yourself and stand your ground with Galatians 5:1, "It is for freedom that Christ has set us free. Stand firm, then, and do not let yourselves be burdened again by a yoke of slavery." Those surveyors can huff, and they can puff, but they cannot blow your house down, because when the Holy Spirit takes over and transforms your life, the demons that used to ding-dong-ditch your front door, waiting for you to open it to see who's there, will be *running* when you unsheathe the sword you so expertly know how to use. Remember, there's only one way to be sure the battle is won: *don't let up until the enemy can't get up.*

I chased my enemies and caught them;

I did not stop until they were conquered.

I struck them down so they could not get up;

they fell beneath my feet. (Psalm 18:37–38 [NLT])

TACTICAL TRAINING

Drill In

Read: Mark 9:25

Reflect: When Jesus cast out the evil spirit from the little boy, He said, "I command you to come out of this child and never enter him again!" If deliverance was final for a lifetime, why would Jesus need to tell a spirit to never return?

Again, we cannot expect rebellious spirits to not rebel. Jesus taught on returning spirits, and He handled those spirits in His deliverances by forbidding them to return!

Read: Matthew 12:43–45

Reflect: The Message version uses the phrase, "old haunt". While we want to cast out devils and do what Jesus did (command them to never return) we also need to be prepared to stand our ground against rebellious spirits who are working in coordination to return to a previous haunt.

Be filled with the Holy Spirit and the gospel of Jesus Christ, keep your doors shut, and command returning spirits to leave and not return.

Read: Ephesians 6:13–14

Reflect: Paul tells us to stand firm and then mentions the belt of truth and breastplate of righteousness.

How might these two pieces of armor help us stand firm against the Devil's schemes?

Drill Out

You have total authority in Jesus Christ to overcome all the power of the enemy. You also have spiritual alertness to handle business and command spirits to never return. Here's the reality of spiritual warfare: we are dealing with stubborn demonic forces, and we know rebellious spirits will attempt to resist and rebel. When this happens, we don't question our authority—we assert it. I pray you crush the enemy so hard that he's unable to get back up and try again.

However, if you experience a returning visitor, don't panic, and don't give up. The only way rebellious spirits know you're serious is when you show them.

If you experience any spirits trying to bounce back, go back into your strategic prayer plan and wipe them out! If they try to get back into their old house, tell them, "I'm not your house anymore, and the Holy Spirit reigns here!"

Drill Down

Colossians 1:6

CHAPTER 14

Roll Call

It's time to hit your beat. "Beat" is cop talk for a patrol area. When an officer is "on the beat" this means they're out patrolling their assigned area. The term is said to be derived from the phrase "beaten path", because day after day, you maintain law and order in the area assigned to you. The enemy is a menace, working to steal, kill, and destroy, which is why we have to patrol our beat and keep him where he belongs—under our authority in Christ (Luke 10:19). Before officers go on their beat, they sit down for something termed "roll call". Roll call is a briefing conducted prior to the start of a shift where officers check in with their unit, inspect uniforms, load equipment, and share information to recap the latest incidents and what to expect on the streets. In other words, roll call is essential to ensure officers are informed, equipped, and prepared before they go on their beats. It's time for you to hit your beat and start splintering these strongholds. Are you ready to *take captives and make arrests* from your hit list (2 Corinthians 10:5)? Do it like the pros.

Before heading out on your own, let's recap the essentials with a short briefing.

WEAPONS FOR WHAT?

We are in a spiritual battle, and we have spiritual defenses (Ephesians 6:10–18).

- 2 Corinthians 10:4 tells us we have been given weapons of warfare that are not carnal, but mighty through God for the tearing down of strongholds.

- Our weapons of warfare drive us to pull down, cast down, and bring into captivity.

- While the armor of God equips us with pieces for offense and defense, it's our weapons of warfare that provide a means for militant attack.

- If this is what we have been equipped with, one should assume we'll actually need the equipment.

- We are not defenseless in this battle; therefore, we should defend ourselves.

- Here's the good news: we have spiritual defenses for a spiritual battle.

THE STARTING LINE: "ON YOUR MARKS"

Let's make sure your starting line is where it needs to be.

- Do not attempt without Christ's love and power.

- His love makes you complete in the fullness of life and power (Ephesians 3:18–19 [NLT]).

- Christ's love in you is the conductor for His power in you.

- You need to know Christ to use His all-powerful name.

Get into a good position to deal with the enemy.

- Deal with the "self" first.

- Deal with the sin of the flesh before you deal with the enemy.

- Use the tactics in this book to battle strongholds of sin.

Don't be the chicken.

- Resist the Devil.

- Someone is going down, and it's not going to be you.

- Resisting is not passive; it is violent opposition.

- When the going gets tough, stick to the plan. Keep resisting.

- Wear him out, hold the line!

DELIVERANCE IS A MIRACLE

Jesus was sent to set the captives free.

- Deliverance follows as a sign of the believer.

- Deliverance was central to Christ's mission, and an equal part of the miracle branch, along with healing, signs, and wonders!

- If you are a believer, deliverance is part of your job. Mark 16:17 includes it in the job description.

- Compassion drives us toward deliverance, even in the face of unbelief and skepticism.

- The Lord works in signs, including deliverance, all for the purpose of confirming His word, and He does this by working with us (Mark 16:20).

- Don't expect a rebellious spirit not to rebel. You will encounter stubborn spirits and strongholds. When this happens, remember, in order to do the Lord's work, we have to work with the Lord. Go back to Him for training, instruction, and keys for breakthrough.

UNSHEATHE THE SWORD

When you need a weapon, begin with God's Word!

- The Word of God is not like a sword, it is a sword.

- God's Word is a weapon that delivers quick and mighty blows!

- Don't fall for the cheap shot. When the Devil tempts us in our flesh, this is his cheap shot.

- Carry the sword on your person. Memorize scripture, embed it in your spirit, and train to unsheathe it quickly.

- We unsheathe it when we speak it.

- Use scripture to identify your targets. "Does this sound like freedom, authority, power, love, and a sound mind?" If the answer is no, it has to go.

- Know your target and use scripture as your ammunition.

THE PERFECT SACRIFICE

Defeat the enemy with the triple threat.

- Command your rights by speaking the name. Enforce your rights by pleading the blood. Remember your rights by partaking in communion.

- Because of His body that was given, His blood that was shed, and His name that was exalted, we have mighty weapons and tactics that make strongholds go *BOOM!*

- Christ died to set you free from every form of slavery. This is not an empty promise, it is guaranteed. You don't have to beg for something that is guaranteed. John 8:36 puts it this way, "So if the Son sets you free, you will be free indeed."

- There is no higher name than the name of Jesus, and we have been given His name. Demons submit to His name.

- Jesus explained the qualifications for who can use His name—anyone who believes. He announced, "And these signs shall follow them that believe; In my name shall they cast out devils…" (Mark 16:17 [KJV]). According to Jesus, anyone who believes in Christ can use His name to cast out devils, and this is a sign that naturally follows the believer.

- He died for you to have total freedom! When you plead the blood of Christ, you enforce your rights to freedom by using the blood of Christ as your defense! This is a powerful practice that will keep you standing firm against any lie from the enemy that you're not truly free.

- Taking communion fortifies the believer because we remember Jesus paid the price for our freedom, and now we have life in abundance.

- Don't incriminate yourself by pleading the thorn; plead the blood!

BRING OUT THE BATTERING RAM

Dealing with a stronghold? Need help? Fasting is a head-turner in Heaven.

- Your victory is in proportion to the display of your desperation.

- Jesus told us that to overcome stubborn demons, we must activate prayer and fasting.

- If you have problems with the soul or flesh, fasting afflicts the soul, crucifies it, and redirects the chain of command to the spirit.

- Our weapons of warfare are not carnal, but they are mighty in God. Fasting is the least carnal thing you can do. Fasting decreases how much you are operating in your carnality because as you deny yourself fuel, your human strength weakens. This is the point of fasting, you come to depend on God's strength and not your own.

- When you fast correctly your voice is heard on high.

- When you fast in a way that pleases God, you can expect things to break forth suddenly, to appear quickly, and to receive God's help, protection, and His personal reply.

- Fasting was often deployed as a response in times of warfare and distress because it is a warfare tactic and weapon.

WHOOP IN PRAYER

Pray with boldness, but remember these essentials.

- Put on the armor of God.
- Be strengthened in the Lord.
- Know where you sit (with Christ!)
- Agree with God's plans and purposes.
- Stay under the covering.
- Stay under the heeding and leading.
- Repent and renounce.
- Decree and declare.
- Bind and loose.
- Deal with the first and strongest: the doorman and strongman.

THE POWER OF A PLAN

Whatever you do… do NOT abandon the plan!

- When the enemy tries to keep you on the merry-go-round, having a plan will keep you steady and focused.

- Don't be bullied by false highs and false hopes. Go for the victory!

- Leave no survivors, clear the land!

- Use scripture as your weapon, not your crutch.

- Resisting the Devil requires a militant approach. Resisting is not hands off. It's sleeves up and earrings off.

DEALING WITH RETURN VISITORS

Jesus forbid returning spirits, so don't let them harass you.

- The reason the evil spirit was able to reclaim his old home was because the man was not hospitable to the Kingdom message (Matthew 12:43–45 [MSG]).

- You must occupy yourself with the gospel of Jesus Christ and become filled with the Holy Spirit.

- Do not allow returning spirits to cause you to question your freedom.

- Stand your ground and make them go.

- Forbid them to return.

- Keep your doors shut.

THE FINAL CHARGE

Dear Overcomer,

What a journey it has been. Thank you for allowing me to walk with you. It has been a privilege and honor to encourage you as you stand firmly in your authority as a believer.

I leave you here, but don't worry, your Advocate is right beside you. You have a mighty General to lead you to victory in Christ. Do you know His name? Immanuel, God with us (Matthew 1:23). He is the God of breakthrough (2 Samuel 5:20).

Overcomer, you've been busy. You've done the hard work to identify your targets, practice your biblical tactics, and load your weapons with scriptural ammunition. Well done! *Boot camp has been fun!*

But now the real work begins. You have an enemy to overcome. Stick to the plan and press in with your militant prayer strategy.

My final charge to you?

Don't leave any outstanding warrants.

Take captives, make arrests, and make strongholds go BOOM.

Be free (John 8:36).

Appendix

Within the pages of this Appendix, you will find worksheets and handouts designed to help you use your biblical weapons of warfare to tear down strongholds. *If you'd like a printable worksheet to write on, you can find one at carastarns.com.*

I. Shotgun Sniper Worksheet

II. Hit List

III. Example Shotgun Sniper Worksheet and Prayer

IV. How to Take Communion

DEFEND YOURSELF

THE SHOTGUN SNIPER WORKSHEET

SEE A STRONGHOLD
MAKE IT GO BOOM!

It's time to be **tactful**. This is where your weapons of warfare will come together in prayer to destroy strongholds. You will use these sections to mark your targets, load your ammo, and execute a militant plan to overcome the enemy. Do this daily for as long as needed. Remember the mission.

Don't stop until the enemy is conquered (Psalm 18:37–38). (See the example prayer on pages 286-289)

1. Mark Your Targets

What are you targeting? List it here. Use scripture to identify your targets. "Does this sound like freedom, authority, power, love, and a sound mind?" If the answer is no, it has to go.

EX: Spirit of fear, spirit of infirmity, etc. (See the "Hit List" in the appendix for more.)

_____

_____

_____

_____

_____

_____

_____

_____

_____

2. Load Your Ammo

What scripture will you be standing on to disarm the Devil and defend your faith? Use scripture as your ammunition. Write out the full verses unless you have them memorized and get out a journal if you need additional pages!

EX: Disarm the spirit of fear with 2 Timothy 1:7, Isaiah 43:1, Psalm 23:4, etc.

EX: Defend your faith that God comes when you call and He saves you with Lamentations 3:57, Psalm 57:3, etc.

APPENDIX

DEFEND YOURSELF

3. Persist In Prayer!

Write down a prayer to lead you in your daily contending. In this prayer, you will want to speak the WORD, use the NAME, and plead the BLOOD. You will want to REPENT, RENOUNCE, BIND, AND LOOSE. Don't leave anything behind.

Focus on using language such as:

"I repent of _____." (Repent of sins, open doors, agreeing with lies or demonic assignments, etc.)

"I break every agreement I've made with the spirit of _____."

"I renounce all ways I have partnered with, agreed with, or opened doors to _____."

"I repent before the Lord for _____ and ask for forgiveness."

"I cancel the assignment of _____ in the name of Jesus."

"In the name of Jesus, I destroy any legal rights the spirit of _____ may have through _____."

"I come out of agreement with _____ and come into agreement with the Word of God, which says, _____."

"I plead the blood of Jesus over me, over my mind!"

APPENDIX

"I bind _____."

"I loose _____."

"I sever every tie with _____."

"I declare Christ has set me free. By His power, I am loosed from every evil spirit, and I command every evil spirit to leave me now, I cast you out in the mighty name of Jesus!"

"I forbid any evil spirits to return, not under old assignments or new ones."

"I decree and declare the power of _____ is defeated in my life now!"

"I crucify these areas of my flesh: _____."

"I surrender _____ to Jesus."

"I declare the fruits of the Holy Spirit (_____) will now flourish in my life."

"I come into agreement with God's word and I declare I am set free from _____."

"I come into agreement with God's Word and I declare _____." (i.e. I have a sound mind)

"I take the blood of Jesus and plead His merciful blood over my life, I declare His blood has made me clean, as white as snow (1 Peter 1:19) and I apply the blood of Jesus to every door that has been opened, and I now shut it and decree it to remain shut in the name of Jesus."

APPENDIX

4. Know your strategy and make the plan

When will you pray? (Every morning, every evening, etc.)

_____

_____

_____

How will you fast? Pray about what to fast, and how long and often to fast. (One day a week, three whole days, one meal a day, water fast, all food, "choice" foods, etc.)

_____

_____

_____

_____

_____

_____

Put it all together

- ✶ Speak the WORD
- ✶ Use the NAME
- ✶ Plead the BLOOD
- ✶ Remember through COMMUNION
- ✶ Breakthrough with FASTING
- ✶ Whoop in PRAYER

HIT LIST

Identify Your Targets

Ask the Holy Spirit to lead you in identifying any spirits that need to be dealt with. As they are revealed, add them to the target section of your worksheet. When it's time to prepare your prayer, use scripture to specifically address these spirits, and aim for the bullseye!

You'll want to repent of sins, and when you do, be sure to use this list to identify the spirits behind that sin. While stealing is a sin, behind it could be the spirit of greed, the spirit of mental illness and addiction (kleptomania), or the spirit of rebellion. Repent of the sin and work with the Holy Spirit to identify the spirit behind it. Remember, spirits come in packs to throw a house party. Even if you feel like a spirit has a small hand in your life, go ahead and include it in your Hit List. It's better to be thorough now.

When it comes to illness, maybe this is another stronghold over your life. The woman that Jesus healed in Luke 13 was crippled by a spirit for eighteen years (Luke 13:11). Usually, when a sick person was presented to Jesus, He laid hands on them and healed them. In this story, though, Jesus addressed a demonic spirit behind the illness. He told the woman, "Be loosed of thine infirmity!". He cast out the spirit, then He laid hands on her and healed her. In this case, Christ healed a woman, but first He had to cast out the evil spirit. When you come to strongholds in your life of physical and mental illness, simply ask the Holy Spirit what to do. If you're not sure, apply your faith and authority. Write this in the prayer section of your worksheet, "In the mighty name of Jesus, I decree and declare that by the stripes of Jesus I am healed of (insert the illness). In the name of Jesus, I cast out the spirit of infirmity and I release God's redemption and healing over my body."

Some people are able to take care of business through strategic prayer, while others will need help from experienced ministers. If you have severe trauma, a history in the occult or new age practices, or overwhelming torments, you might want to contact an experienced minister to work with you through your journey. You can look for ministers in your area using Isaiah Saldivar's "Deliverance Map" at isaiahsaldivar.com/deliverance.

- Abandonment
- Addiction
- Adultery
- Anger
- Anxiety
- Apathy
- Arrogance
- Bitterness
- Control
- Criticism
- Death
- Depression
- Discouragement
- Disease
- Doubt
- Envy
- Fear
- Fornication
- Greed
- Guilt
- Hatred
- Haughtiness
- Heaviness
- Homosexuality

- Hopelessness
- Hysteria
- Impatience
- Inadequacy
- Ineptness
- Insomnia
- Jealousy
- Judgment
- Lying
- Manipulation
- Mental Illness
- Mind-binding
- Murder
- Occult
- Perversion
- Phobias
- Pride
- Rebellion
- Rejection
- Resentment
- Self-centeredness
- Self-condemnation
- Self-hatred
- Selfishness
- Self-pity
- Self-rejection
- Shame
- Sickness
- Strife
- Sorcery
- Stubbornness
- Suicide
- Timidity
- Trauma
- Retaliation
- Witchcraft
- Worry
- Unforgiveness
- Unworthiness
- Violence

EXAMPLE WORKSHEET AND PRAYER

My Targets:

- ✖ Spirit of fear (doorman)
- ✖ Spirit of death (strongman)
- ✖ Spirit of anxiety—overthinking, stress, panic attacks, neck tension, stomach pain, etc.
- ✖ Spirit of heaviness
- ✖ Footholds to die to self on—criticism, apathy, impatience, arrogance, pride, and hate.

My Ammo:

- (1) Philippians 2:9–10
- (2) Isaiah 53:5
- (3) Romans 12:3
- (4) Isaiah 26:3
- (5) Psalm 27:1
- (6) Deuteronomy 31:8
- (7) Galatians 2:20
- (8) 2 Corinthians 1:9
- (9) 2 Corinthians 5:8
- (10) Psalm 118:17
- (11) Isaiah 41:10
- (12) Psalm 91:15
- (13) Isaiah 43:1
- (14) Psalm 28:7
- (15) Psalm 34:4
- (16) 2 Timothy 1:7
- (17) Matthew 16:19
- (18) James 4:7

- (19) Philippians 4:7
- (20) Isaiah 61:3
- (21) Matthew 6:13
- (22) Ephesians 4:21
- (23) Titus 2:12
- (24) Galatians 5:22–23
- (25) Proverbs 2:6
- (26) Ephesians 4:1–6
- (27) Jeremiah 29:11
- (28) Philippians 4:6–8
- (29) Matthew 12:44
- (30) Luke 8:31
- (31) Mark 9:25
- (32) John 8:36
- (33) John 10:10
- (34) Revelation 12:11
- (35) John 14:27
- (36) Hebrews 9:22
- (37) Ephesians 1:7
- (38) Luke 4:18
- (39) Luke 10:19

My Plan:

- ✓ **Execute my strategic prayer in the morning**
- ✓ **Take communion with my morning prayer**
- ✓ **Fast through breakfast and lunch**

My Prayer:

In the name of Jesus—the highest name—I plead His precious blood over me! (1) By His blood, I declare I am healed of trauma and PTSD. By His stripes, I have received everlasting peace to my mind and body. (2) By His blood, I declare my mind is renewed to agree with His Word. (3, 4) There is only ONE stronghold in my life, and it is The Lord, Immanuel—God with me. Whom shall I fear? (5) I will not fear. I will not be dismayed. (6) I bind up the spirit of fear and fear of death. I am not afraid of you. I've already died to myself, and I have eternal life through Christ. (7) So I put my trust in the God who raises the dead. (8) To be absent from the body is to be present with the Lord. The believer doesn't fear death, so by the precious blood of Jesus today I will live and not die. (9, 10) I fear nothing, because God is with me. (11) The Lord comes when I call, I am His. He helps me. (12, 13, 14) He delivers me from every fear and strengthens me with power, love, and a sound mind. (15, 16)

I bind and resist the spirit of anxiety. (17, 18) The peace of God guards my heart and mind against anxiety. (19) I bind up the spirit of heaviness. I resist you and lift my spirit with the garment of praise! (20)

I renounce and break every agreement I've made (knowingly and unknowingly) with the spirits of fear, death, anxiety, heaviness, and every spirit under their authority. I cancel your assignments in the name of Jesus. I render you powerless and your assignments null and void. Lord, deliver me from evil. (21) I renounce all ways I have partnered with or opened doors to the spirit of fear (doorman) to be at work in my life. I command all footholds to be destroyed by the blood of Jesus. In the name of Jesus, I destroy the power of fear in my life now. Jesus, set me free from fear and fear of death (strongman)!

I declare I will not give the Devil a single foothold. (22) I crucify my flesh and repent of criticism, apathy, impatience, arrogance, pride, and hate. I renounce wickedness. (23) Lord, I receive now, by the Holy Spirit, love, joy, peace, patience, kindness, goodness, faithfulness, gentleness, self-control, wisdom, unity, and hope. (24, 25, 26, 27) I declare I will be humble and please the Lord, and I will be anxious about nothing but pray in all occasions and set my mind on what is good and praise worthy. (28)

I submit to God. (18) Now to the spirits of fear, death, anxiety, heaviness, and every spirit under their authority—I rebuke and resist you all. (18) I am not your home! (29) I command you to leave now, I cast you out in the name of Jesus! Go immediately to the pit. (30) In the name of Jesus, I forbid you to return—not under old assignments nor new assignments. (31) And I command you to take your baggage with you. All impacts and manifestations to my mind and body—a racing heart, sick stomach, heavy head, overthinking, brain fog, difficulty breathing, uneven breathing, shortness of breath, burning eyes, dry mouth, tight throat, neck tension, and tight chest—I rebuke and cancel your assignments to destroy my mind and body and I decree and declare I am free! (32) Lord, seal my doors shut with your blood—the blood that speaks of life, peace, forgiveness, redemption, freedom, and authority through Jesus Christ! (33, 34, 35, 36, 37, 38, 39)

Amen.

(Close your prayer by taking communion.)

HOW TO TAKE COMMUNION

When Jesus instructed us to take communion, He modeled the holy act in someone's home. Jesus gave us the precious gift of connecting with Him in our own homes, in a tender moment before we fill our bellies.

If you wish to sit down in your own home and take communion, but you don't have formal elements such as wine or communion crackers, please don't let that stop you. So much of Jesus' ministry was making do with the little that His followers had. He turned water into wine and multiplied a child's few loaves and fishes for the masses.

Pull a Jesus move and use what you have on hand to step into a holy encounter. Be free.

Examine Yourself

First, pause and ask the Holy Spirit to search and examine your heart (1 Corinthians 11:28). Ask the Holy Spirit to reveal any unrepented or unconfessed sin. You can pray along the lines of Psalm 139:23–24, saying, "Search me, God, and know my heart; test me and know my anxious thoughts. See if there is any offensive way in me, and lead me in the way everlasting." Work with the Holy Spirit to take care of anything He reveals to you. Then, set your heart on Jesus.

Remember Him

Reflect on the sacrifice of Jesus Christ. Remember His blood that was poured out for you. Remember His body that was given for you. Remember that His blood is the new covenant, forgiving your sins, saving you, and giving you eternal life with Christ. Thank Him for His sacrifice, His love, His grace, mercy, and forgiveness. Surrender everything to Him.

> *For I received from the Lord what I also passed on to you: The Lord Jesus, on the night he was betrayed, took bread, and when he had given thanks, he broke it and said, 'This is my body, which is for you; do this in remembrance of me.' In the same way, after supper he took the cup, saying, 'This cup is the new covenant in my blood; do this, whenever you drink it, in remembrance of me.' (1 Corinthians 11:23–25)*

Eat the Bread

First, hold the bread in your hand, which represents His body. (If you don't have bread, any food will do, such as a cracker.) Say a prayer, thank Him for His body, or declare truths according to His sacrifice. Ask the Holy Spirit to help you pray. I might pray,

> *Lord, thank You for Your body that was given for me. Lord, You were the perfect sacrifice, the final sacrifice. I have been sanctified through the sacrifice of the body of Jesus Christ once for all (Hebrews 10:10). Now, I am free. Because of You my sins are forgiven. I am free from death and have eternal life with You. I am Yours.*

Drink the Wine

Next, hold the wine (or any liquid) which represents His blood poured out for you. I might pray,

> *Lord, thank You that Your blood is the new covenant, a covenant that is everlasting. By Your blood, I can enter the Most Holy Place with confidence (Hebrews 10:19). Thank You that Your blood seals the covenant between me and God, forgiving me of my sins (Matthew 26:27–28). I have peace through the blood (Colossians 1:20). I have redemption through the blood (Ephesians 1:7). I am holy through the blood (Hebrews 13:12). I am justified by the blood (Romans 5:9). Your blood cleanses my conscience from sinful acts that hinder me from serving God. I am blood bought, so I declare I will serve the Living God without hindrance (Acts 20:28, Hebrews 9:14)! I am atoned for and have eternal life through the blood of Jesus (Leviticus 17:11). Lord, thank You that Your blood makes me triumph over the enemy (Revelation 12:11). Lord, thank You that by the blood I am redeemed from living an empty way of life (1 Peter 1:18–19). Lord, thank You that I am in You and You are in me (John 6:55–59).*

Conclude

Enforce your freedom and victory in Christ. I might pray,

> *Jesus, I know You died to set me free from slavery so that I would never have to go back to any form of it (Galatians 5:1). So I declare I am free indeed (John 8:36)! I will not become a slave again. Lord, I also know that when You died and rose again, You were given the highest name, and every demon must bow to Your name (Philippians 2:9). Thank You that I was given Your name to cast out devils, heal the sick, and do great miracles for Your glory and to fulfill Your will on earth as it is in Heaven (Mark 16:17–18, Matthew 6:10). Thank You, Lord, for the authority to overcome all the power of the enemy (Luke 10:19). Thank You, Lord, for the authority to command healings, deliverances, peace, miracles, and even unusual miracles. I thank You that my prayers are powerful and effective, and I have total victory in You, Christ Jesus (James 5:16)!*
>
> *Amen*

About the Author

Cara Starns is a minister, evangelist, and podcast host with a heart to see people walk in freedom and intimacy with Christ. She is also the Founder and President of Safe Passage, a nonprofit that combats child trafficking through prevention, mentorship, and support services. (Safepassageky.org) She has a bachelor's degree in International Studies from the University of Kentucky. She has a passion to equip churches around the world to walk in the signs of the believer and carry on the work of Jesus. Cara is from Lexington, KY. You can connect with her and find more resources at carastarns.com

I want to hear your testimony and prayer requests!

Message or tag me on social media: @carastarns

References

Barna Group, Ltd. "Most American Christians Do Not Believe that Satan or the Holy Spirit Exist" (April 13, 2009)." Accessed September 23, 2022. https://www.barna.com/research/most-american-christians-do-not-believe-that-satan-or-the-holy-spirit-exist.

Cedarmont Kids. "I'm In The Lord's Army (YouTube video, October 17, 2013)." Accessed September 23, 2022. https://youtu.be/nJoB5XCQ5gs.

Dailey, Jim. "The Reality of Spiritual Warfare: A Conversation With Tony Evans" (*Decision Magazine*, January 24, 2005)." Accessed September 23, 2022. https://decisionmagazine.com/the-reality-of-spiritual-warfare.

Derocher, Matthew. "In the Lord's Army? (August 03, 2021)." Accessed September 23, 2022. https://theformer.faith/en/post/in-the-lord-s-army.

Eivaz, Jennifer. "Can Physical Ailments Have Spiritual Roots? (December 18, 2019)." Accessed September 23, 2022. https://www.jennifereivaz.com/post/can-physical-ailments-have-spiritual-roots

Eivaz, Jennifer. *Inner Healing and Deliverance Handbook: Hope to Bring Your Heart Back to Life.* Minneapolis, Chosen Books, 2022.

Eivaz, Jennifer, "Jennifer Eivaz: The Praying Prophet". https://www.jennifereivaz.com.

Gatson, Brandon. "School of Reform: Presenting Christ to the Culture but Re-Presenting Christ to the Church". https://schoolofreform.com.

Jones, Timothy. *Extreme Sheep: Experiencing Listening Prayer.* Self-Published, Amazon KDP, 2018.

LeStrange, Ryan, "Atlanta Global Hub", https://www.atlhubchurch.com.

LexisNexis. "The Top 3 Rules of Cross-Examination. (May 20, 2022)." Accessed September 23, 2022. https://www.lexisnexis.com/community/insights/legal/law-books/b/law-books/posts/the-top-3-rules-of-cross-examination#:~:text=What%20Is%20Cross%20Examination%3F,or%20extend%20testimony%20already%20given.

Prince, Derek. "How to Be Delivered." How To Be Delivered | Sermon | Derek Prince Ministries. Accessed September 23, 2022. https://www.derekprince.com/sermons/207.

Renner, Rick. "You Have a Two-Edged Sword (N.D.)." Accessed September 23, 2022. https://renner.org/article/you-have-a-two-edged-sword.

Saldivar, Isaiah. "Deliverance Map." Accessed September 23, 2022. https://www.isaiahsaldivar.com/deliverance.

Saldivar, Isaiah. "Revival Lifestyle Podcast". https://revivallifestyle.libsyn.com.

Saldivar, Isaiah. "Revival Through My Eyes." https://www.isaiah-saldivar.com.

Solomon, Shamel. "I Am Shameless." https://www. shamelsolomon.com.

Soroski, Jason. "The Magnificent Truth in the Command 'Do This in Remembrance of Me' (July 19, 2020)." Accessed September 23, 2022. https://www.biblestudytools.com/bible-study/topical-studies/the-magnificent-truth-in-the-command-do-this-in-remembrance-of-me.html.

van der Kolk, Bessel. *The Body Keeps the Score: Brain, Mind, and Body in the Healing of Trauma.* Reprint Edition. Penguin Publishing Group, 2015.

Van Schaack, Beth. "Siege Warfare and the Starvation of Civilians as a Weapon of War and War Crime (February 4, 2016)." Accessed September 23, 2022. https://www.justsecurity.org/29157/siege-warfare-starvation-civilians-war-crime.